ADVANCE PRAISE

"The power to recognize yourself and accept yourself is one of the most difficult and self-sustaining skills that we all have. Iona shows just how needed and possible it can be."

—VIVEK KEMP, EXECUTIVE PRODUCER, *VICE NEWS*

"Ghost is a haven. In reckoning with her own murderous history with food and shame, Iona Holloway, a narrative sister of Glennon Doyle and Mary Karr, extends a hand down into the pit for her reader. Women who approach the mirror as their judge and enemy, read this. Women who 'have it all' and still hate themselves, read this. Women raising daughters, girls who shouldn't grow up questioning the acceptability of their bodies, read this."

—KAREN VALBY, AUTHOR, *WELCOME TO UTOPIA*

"In Ghost, Holloway explores the devastating consequences of when talent, perfectionism, and overworking collide. She also teaches you how to pick up the pieces and rebuild."

—JASON FEIFER, EDITOR-IN-CHIEF, *ENTREPRENEUR*

"Iona Holloway's book, Ghost, evokes the palpable anxiety, despair, and longing that so many women feel in twenty-first century America. She uses the metaphor of ghosts in a way that resonates and ultimately will help readers find elements of their own experience in Holloway's raw descriptions. Ultimately the message here is hopeful: You can find your strength rather than sink under the weight of societal expectations and prohibitions. You can unlearn the terrible lessons society teaches you and find your Self with a capital S."

—HARRIET BROWN, AUTHOR, *BRAVE GIRL EATING:*
A FAMILY'S STRUGGLE WITH ANOREXIA

"Iona's book, Ghost, provides a gut-wrenching, empowering raw reality check of the pain that exists behind many thin brittle bodies that our culture tends to painfully idolize as beautiful. This book could be the key that allows the skeletons of our dark closets to be seen and freed with strength and acceptance as a first step to self-love."

—CARLI BLAU, NYC SEX AND RELATIONSHIP THERAPIST

"Part memoir, part manifesto, this book acts as a written work of Kintsugi, the Japanese art of repairing broken pottery by mending the breaks with gold and reminding us that our imperfections make us strong, beautiful, and exist as things to celebrate—not hide. Artist, athlete, writer, and warrior, Iona Holloway takes readers on a raw journey to earn the world's attention, praise, and love by dominating her body through restricted eating and excessive exercise. But then she takes the lessons of that journey and creates a road map to recovery for others to follow, offering insights, observations, and hard-won understanding. Holloway is not your standard storyteller, and this is not your standard eating disorder recovery book. And that is a blessing."

—MELISSA CHESSHER, CHAIR AND
PROFESSOR, SYRACUSE UNIVERSITY

"For decades it seems my brain continually races at the same speed of an Olympian who is in the final five meters of a qualifying race. Ghost captures this moment and so many others with beautiful honesty, unapologetic clarity, and without trepidation. I can see myself in Holloway's words and hear my thoughts take a pause, as I truly understand that I am not alone in the world. Thank you for allowing me and all women to be seen."

—LESLIE WINGO, PRESIDENT/CEO, SANDERS/WINGO

"It's fitting that Holloway's memoir is called Ghost, because it's a haunting tale of women shrinking themselves in a desperate bid to feel strong. Her triumph is breathtaking."

—KAT GORDON, FOUNDER AND CEO OF
THE 3 PERCENT MOVEMENT

"In writing Ghost, Iona Holloway has given countless women a great gift: an escape route from the cult of competence. So many intelligent, creative, strong-minded women have polished themselves until there is nothing left. We focus so intently on finding the perfect words and ideas that we begin to believe no word or idea could ever be good enough. Holloway's words have a visceral weight, as if they embody all the parts of herself she spent years shedding and shrinking. The reader is encouraged to take her own journey back in time, to acknowledge how she was abandoned, and what she abandoned on the cutting room floor. Ghost is a full-bodied, full-minded affirmation of need, and a reclamation of everything it means to be alive in your own skin."

—FRANCES DODDS, DIGITAL FEATURES
DIRECTOR, ENTREPRENEUR

"Iona's writing is deeply personal while simultaneously encapsulating the universal experiences of powerful women. *Ghost* offered the empathy—and the hard truths—I needed to continue my own journey toward self-awareness and healing."

—CHRISTINA STERBENZ, SENIOR EDITOR, *VICE NEWS*

"Iona's work consistently inspires me to be vulnerable and introspective with myself and bring a more whole self to my external world."

—REBECCA SANANES, PODCAST PRODUCER, *NEW YORK MAGAZINE*

"Iona shares the haunting truth of how our younger experiences can shape perfectionism and emotional numbness, creating the perfect path towards starving, stuffing, and exercising on repeat. *Ghost* is a poetic look into the shadows of many women's experiences with disordered eating and the pursuit of thinness. I found myself gripped by the resonance of, 'I've been there too,' as I read the sometimes jarring words Iona shares. *Ghost* doesn't leave us without wisdom on how to move forward though. There are vital pieces to the painfully beautiful journey back home to ourselves, offered in these pages."

—RICHELLE LUDWIG, SOMATIC COACH

"*Ghost* beautifully and authentically articulates the pain of living in a body striving to be small, both literally and figuratively. Holloway explores the body wars so many women fight with an honesty and bravery that is visceral. *Ghost* is both a piece of art and a powerful healing resource for women who have ever felt like they are 'too much' or 'not enough.' All women who have fought with food and their body will feel seen and heard by this book."

—TRACI CARSON, PHD CANDIDATE, PUBLIC HEALTH

"I first admired Iona Holloway as a bright, creative ambitious grad student. Her work bordered on flawless. Later I admired her for her strength, discipline, and dedication as a competitive weight lifter. But now, more importantly, I admire her as a woman able to tell her true story, admit her regrets, and share the struggles she coped with all because so many of us did see her as perfect, when, of course, she wasn't."

—EDWARD BOCHES, PROFESSOR OF ADVERTISING/
CREATIVE DIRECTOR/AUTHOR

"Having had the privilege of knowing Iona throughout her graduate studies, I would expect nothing less than this bold, powerful, and brutally honest piece of work. In Ghost, she lays bare her experiences and feelings to hopefully help other women deal with theirs."

—PEGEEN RYAN, ASSOCIATE PROFESSOR OF
THE PRACTICE, BOSTON UNIVERSITY

GHOST

ghost

WHY PERFECT WOMEN SHRINK

iona holloway

LIONCREST
PUBLISHING

GHOST
Why Perfect Women Shrink

ISBN   978-1-5445-1719-3   *Hardcover*
         978-1-5445-1718-6   *Paperback*
         978-1-5445-1717-9   *Ebook*

Illustrations by Laura Tanguay.

For my niece, Evie

Never disappear

Contents

MAKE YOURSELF REAL

"We are all the places in the wood. Even though no one is here now, the wood is dense with memories where the grass has been trampled down an infinite number of times. We are the places where the words fell, life-giving and life-destroying and paralyzing and uplifting.

We are the long, gliding hours, and all the places. At every step, there is a memorial. If they were visible, we would appear as one ghostly web of life."

—*THE BRIDGES*, TARJEI VESAAS

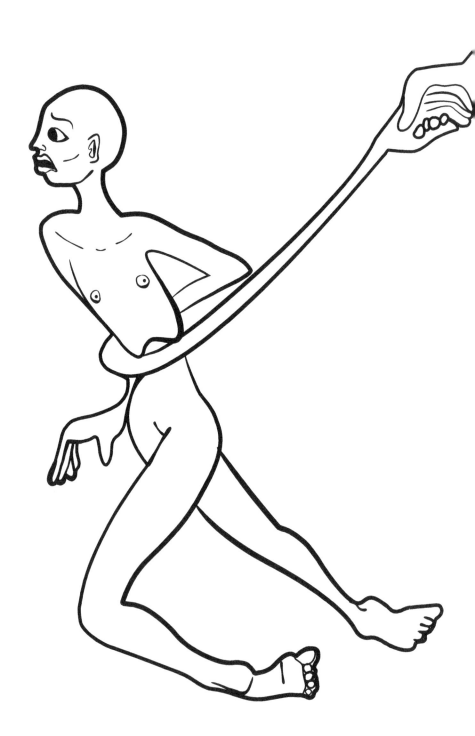

I see you

———

You're hungry
I know
You're hunting
In the wrong place
I thought it was about bones
About small
Now I see
All I was hungry for
All these years
Was someone
Anyone
To ask
How are you really
And for me
To feel safe
Saying
I am not good

WOMEN LIKE US

Women like us. There is no one way we come to exist in this world. Some of us are starving. Some of us are stuffing. Some of us are shining. Some of us are hiding. Some of us are victims. Some of us are lucky. Some speak loudly. Some are silent. Some of us have families. Some don't know our father's smell.

Our lives are not carbon copies. You have your own flavour of pain. Many broken roads lead to the same cruel moment.

So hear these words. Feel it in your bones. Know what is true about a woman like you. A woman like me.

Women like us.

We're everything they said we would be. From the moment we dropped out of the womb showing an uncanny ability to master just about anything. We are the child who takes care of herself. We grow stiff in your arms. We grow into the kid so competent no one offers a hand—or a hug. No one worries about us. *Bookmark her for greatness.* Our tears mean a little less. What have we got to cry about? We learn to swallow it down and work. Our gifts make our pain invisible. We sit quietly behind the couch and wonder: *why don't they see what I feel?*

Women like us. We put our parents on edge from the day we ask a question they do not want to answer. Contrary. Quietly nodding. *She's different from the rest.* They try to answer our questions safely. But our elastic brain has already wrapped itself around the next puzzle to make them feel useless, mere bystanders to our plots and dreams.

We grow up. Into the women no one asks about. Not because we are not loved and admired. *Because* we are loved and admired. The assumption is that whatever we're doing, we do not need help. So we learn. *I am on my own.*

Women like us. We're everything those watching thought we could be. We're everything they wish they were. Diligent. Militant. A glint of crazy and blue-blooded, a heart of coal. The hot and sweaty belly of summer can't melt our ice.

You see us on city streets. *Get out of our way.* We walk in straight lines. We're careful about who we smile at. We worship our full-length mirrors or close our eyes and zoom past. Rumbling stomachs let us know when we're doing it right. It does not matter if our jeans cut into our hips. It keeps the bite of hunger at bay. The numbers hum, and we count the calories in lettuce to make sure we keep our bodies pointed.

They comment on our discipline. It washes over us like balm on crusty lips, easing the discomfort for a moment. So we learn: *small* gets me the words I crave.

Women like us. We're barely seen as women. People always listen to what we have to say. Even the bald men with dumb jokes, because they know we mean business. Our families don't know when to call. So they don't. They assume we're doing fine. *Not just fine.* We're winning. At everything, prize or no prize. Whether we break our backs in the process or not. For women like us, pain means we're doing it right.

Women like us. We are not practiced in love, but we floor men and women with our wit. Like flies to a corpse. Delicious in every way. They tell their friends: *She's not like other women.* Not needy. Not insecure. So we learn: *they only love me strong.*

Women like us. We're fucking remarkable. A once in a lifetime kind of woman. Those close to us feel it, because we make sure they feel it. So they sink into the couch. They pale in our shadow and rest on our backbone. We will be damned if we show how much their ordinariness weighs on us.

And this armour is not built gently. Alarm off. Shoes on. Our skin is hot and wet with sweat before the cold sun bothers rising.

The normal people. They don't dare look us in the eye. Our tenor rips through their flimsy feelings. Our stare chills their average thoughts. They do exactly what we want them to do. They stare straight through us and see exactly what we want them to see. *Perfect.*

BARELY HUMAN

Women like us. We're the one everyone watches, but no one sees. From the moment we were born, we had no reason to cry. They assumed we did not need a hand. They didn't see when we had to start working. They think everything we do is effortless.

Being the one no one asks about is not a good thing.

Not overnight, but we become their lie.

Tangled in the web.

I don't struggle.

I am perfect.

So we make how hard we work invisible. We get good at playing out the lies. They get good at drinking in the lies, like warm and hearty milk. It keeps them sleepy and quiet to our truth.

Women like us. In all our brilliance. In all our strength and in all our gifts. Our humanity disappears. That's why we must keep moving, hunted by their eyes and a hunger that bites and feeds on our fear. Eyes flinty and focused on the horizon.

Women like us. Everything we do must position us above. Not on par, and never below. We cannot lay our head. Not for one moment. Because if we rest, we get comfortable. We get fat and sloppy and whiny. Like everybody else.

We cannot stop. If we stop, our smokescreen dissolves. They'll see what we really feel. Who we really are.

They'll see what we see when we stare through ourselves in the bathroom mirror. A speckling of toothpaste and the stink of fear.

A fucking monster.

When the sun comes up, we are running. We are running through people, their hearts crunching as we stomp. And we are sneering. Sneering at their obvious weakness, and at all the support they need. We're jabbing and poking at how little they believe in themselves. At how worthless their dull lives are.

Arm's length is the measure of choice. We cannot stop. We

cannot rest. The bite of hunger steals our sleep, we wear our eyebags with sick glory. This is what we have to do to keep the truth invisible, so they don't see what we see staring back at us in the mirror.

Fat fuck. Liar. Fraud.

Women like us. They will never see the ways we struggle. They will never realise that what fuels us to soar is not ease but salty and thick fear. The fear of being discovered a fraud.

They will never understand that talent does not mean painless. That competence does not mean effortless. That gifts do not protect us from the rocks that wreck a soul.

They will never see how hard we have been working.

All this time. To them.

We are so perfect, we are nothing.

Barely human.

Immune.

Invisible.

A Ghost.

I see you.

I see straight through you. Not in the way you want, in the way you need. You don't have to be strong here. Because I know your story. It was my story. A different flavour, the same cruel end. No talent, no gift, no tiny number on the scale, and no capacity for work is wide or deep enough to hold you together anymore.

Women like us.

We run from the pain no one else sees.

We are Ghost Women.

We all break in the end.

I need you to know from the bottom of a once empty heart.

You are in the right place.

I'm going to help you come home.

WHY LISTEN TO ME?

I'm Iona. It started off perfect for me, too. I was the child who was good at everything. The precocious talent. Complicated, a little contrary. Hard to wrap your arms around. The one everyone said to watch. And I did it all. I was top of my class. In everything. I won art competitions. I wore my clothes back to front on purpose. I represented my country, Scotland. I was an All American Division I field hockey player at Syracuse University. My grades were ridiculous. Professors loved me. Bosses loved me. I got pay raises without asking. And my body? It stopped people on the street.

I had what they wanted.

I had it all.

And I would go home at night and hope I died in my sleep.

On the surface, I had no reason to feel the way I did. When my star was shining brightest, I felt the scariest feeling in the world.

Nothing.

Nothing, dotted with white hot fear.

I was terrified that people would see how ordinary I really was. So I screamed my invisible pain in the only way that still let me feel strong.

I started to shrink.

For over fifteen years, I waged a war on my body through restriction, bingeing, and over-exercising. And working. A lot of quiet and invisible work.

War served me well. It kept up the appearance everyone expected from me. A formidable force of a woman. My fucked-up relationship with food and my body made me an incredible athlete. It was my job to be extreme. Training for four hours a day was normal. It was so easy to compensate for my binges that grew larger and longer as the years passed. Every time I took a plane ride, I promised myself that when I landed, I would start my life over. That it would be different this time.

It never was.

Year on year on year, it got harder and harder to be me.

My pain hid in plain sight. No one noticed. Or if they did, they said nothing.

They saw what I wanted them to see. *Perfect.*

In my late twenties, I hit an invisible bottom. My whole day centred around the ticking over of calories. I would eat nothing. Then I would eat everything. I could barely drag myself to the gym to make up for my greed. I would sway, standing in the office kitchen weighing kale. My body hurt. My skin hurt. My period was gone.

I thought this was just how it was.

I often dreamed about my funeral.

I thought I was never going to feel better.

But here I stand.

And I want to show you how I got here.

When I was scrabbling around in the dirt trying to get help, I did not see women who looked like me.

Who felt like me. Who spoke like me.

So many flowers and empty words. Pastel colours, script fonts, and 'hey babes.' All I wanted was for someone to call me by my name. And tell me the truth. Unadorned.

I hope in this book you feel seen. Understood. Held. Perhaps for the first time.

This is our story.

It is mine. It is yours.

This is the story of Ghost Women.

The women who lost their humanity a long time ago.

The women whose pain hides in plain sight.

The women who shrink to be visible.

I am going to show you why gifted girls do not get the love they need. Why your competence sets you up to suffer. I'm going to show you how your identity is a web of lies. Spun by others, and then by you. I'm going to show you how *perfect* tied its noose around your neck. Why feeling like a fraud is created by the disconnection of the inside and outside self. I'm going to show you why your pain is invisible to everyone. I'm going to show you why your body became your battlefield. I'm going to show you how to feel real. How to thaw from emotional freeze. To free yourself from shame, blame, and fear. And in witnessing your invisible pain, I'm going to show you how you can heal the women around you and the tiny girls who don't exist yet. I'm going to show you how to bend in the winds of this life. I'm going to show you that you are your wisest teacher. An eternal muse.

I'm going to show you all this using the one thing I know will set you free. It set me free.

Vulnerability.

Vulnerability is the key that unlocked me.

Vulnerability is the key that will unlock you.

This book has bits of my story, and bits of the stories of women I have sat quietly with, listened to, and coached through their own healing. All the women I have taught to start small, and grow tall. It is the story of how to make your pain visible, and in doing so, break free from perfect pain.

BEGIN

No one ever asked me if I was okay.
They assumed I was.
Being the one no one asks about is not a good thing.
I was not fine.
You are not fine.
But you're safe here.
You don't have to be strong.
Or perfect.
Or the best.
Not anymore.
You think you're broken.
You are not broken.
Let me show you how to feel real.
And if the pain feels beyond you.
If the work feels too hard.
Mark these words.
Now is not the time to shrink

—IONA

why you disappear

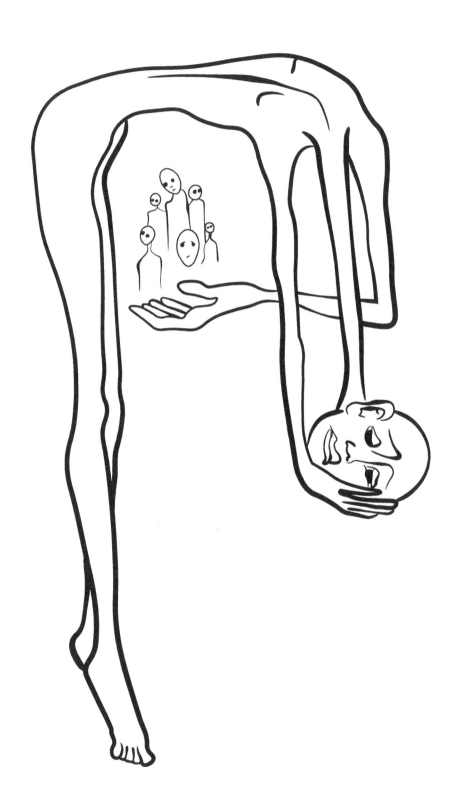

CHAPTER 1

Ghost

WHY YOUR PAIN IS INVISIBLE TO OTHERS

———

I don't know how I got here
But
It's in my hands
The right piece of paper
Tiny handwriting. Lines and scribbles in the margins
Some of the wrong words. Most of the right words
I turn around
The vaulted ceilings
The stained glass
Fake Jesus looks beautiful today
The organ pipes rising up into what could be the clouds
I stare out from the stage
Hundreds of them
Eyes. So many pairs
Lines upon lines of bored eyes
It's the last day of my life
At least it feels like it

The last day of school
I'm giving the head girl's end-of-year speech
These are shoo-ins
Necessary boredom
Pleasantries
But I'm not okay
Last night I wasn't okay either
As I scribbled away
So they're going to hear it
What it's actually like
To be perfect
I start
It does not sound like my voice
Quivering and scared
I plough on
I tell them everything
What it's like to wake up
When you are supposed to be happy
And see nothing
But a monster in the mirror
It's getting quiet in here
Silence hanging in the tall air
I have the ears
I have the room
I have his handkerchief
He's handing it to me
The headmaster
With a look of shock and awe
I'm weeping now
This was not what the head girl was supposed to say
On her last day
In front of the whole school and their parents
That actually

The perfect girl
With the brains
The art
The sport
The gifts
The glory
The girl with the world at her feet
Is fucked up
Inconvenient, isn't it?
To hear the truth
I search for my mum's eyes
I can't see a thing
I stop talking
The room erupts
People are standing
They don't know why
It does not matter
I can't feel a thing
Except my skirt digging into my hip
I slump back to my chair
Flanked by ten trophies
I sit down
I go home
No one mentions it
And I disappear
For another twelve years
Until this book
Until I have the love and the guts to write this book

THE INVISIBLE CHILD

Ghost Women are born without permission to be human. It is not a decision we make for ourselves. It is one made for us in the loud and quiet moments of childhood when we do everything a little too quickly, or too well. Competence is not a desirable trait for a child. When a child learns everything at lightning speed, there is no room for parenting. For learning to be wrong. Smart and quick render us invisible. Rather than being encouraged to act our age, we pull our socks up and press forward into the realities and intricacies of being the one to watch. From day one, the usual rules do not apply. Perfect does.

The assumed competence of Invisible Children is poisonous. Consciously or otherwise, we grow up feeling different. We feel the way parents and grandparents look at us. Head cocked to one side with a look of awed bewilderment. My grandpa would mutter darkly, "That one's been here before," as I disappeared behind the couch to start a new project. The fawning, chuckling teachers. They'd take my mum aside, nodding in my direction. *She's special, that one. Clever cookie.*

We hear them whisper about our gifts. Quietly enough that our heads don't swell and our feet don't grow too big for our boots. We still hear it. And our heart leaps.

I was this child. I loved the feeling. I felt special. Standing out, and alone. I walked at eight months. I would pick up instruments and know how to make music. Tennis racquets, hockey sticks. They fit perfectly in my willful little hands. I ran rings around girls twice my age. Awards, medals, trophies. They stuck to me like glue.

Smart children are gifted an easy life. That is the unspoken undertone. From our parents who leave us alone and compare our aloof brilliance to our normal siblings. Even when they don't mean to. From the parents of other children who watch us glow, casting their darkening eyes down to the average child tangled in their legs.

In historical paintings, children were not portrayed as children but as miniature adults, complete with grown-into faces, breasts, and bodies. Painted at work. Justifying their right to dinner. Invisible Children are no different. Ability artificially shortens our childhood. We grow up too soon. We quickly fool those who watch and admire us. Casting them under the spell of competence. Humanity bleeding out as we shine.

DAZZLE

The Invisible Child has nothing to worry about. That is the silent directive. We're good at everything. Our future is ensured, success guaranteed. On the rare occasions we cry, no one hears us. Our gifts scapegoat us. Invisible Children learn early on to keep quiet about the small ways we struggle. That the tears we shed are not valid, that we should be grateful for the gift of being gifted. We learn early to swallow and to stiffen into our brilliance. We watch as the sweet and gentle children run to their mother and make her feel needed in a way we never will.

Over the years, pressure builds inside the tiny bodies of gifted girls. We are still too young to realise that there are holes in our game. The puzzles, homework, and books we chew through like white bread only reinforce the bath of unspoken expectation we sit in. A bath we are slowly starting to run for ourselves. A bath we will drown in one day.

Invisible Children do not get to feel the sickening thump of failure early on. The aching feeling of not being good enough. The clear setting of limitations. Rules around what we are good at do not exist. We do not learn how to fall apart in front of people, confronted by how useless we are. We have no idea what second place means. What a fat B looks like. Our competence wraps us in cotton wool, protecting us from all the bumps and the bruises the Average Child is smacked with daily. We are weakened by all that makes us good.

The Average Child knows how human they are. They see and feel their incompetence. They fail. They weep. They are hugged. Average Children learn that they are loved in spite of their flaws. There is no weight of expectation. They are told not to worry, born off the hook. Helping hands are endlessly offered and no one assumes they know how to deal with everything alone.

Being an Average Child comes with its own set of challenges. The pain of perfect is not one of them.

Perfect is our mantle. The Invisible Child's unbearable weight. And we dazzle endlessly. How human we are remains untested, we gather no proof of love in spite of failure. The slow grating of struggle remains a mystery to us. An unknown. We encode that the perfect outcome is expected even when nothing but the echoes of our own skull state the pressure.

Those watching us grow to believe we do not need their help.

Our dads don't reach down to pick us up when we look a little lost. Our mums feel shunned by our prickly independence. They don't realise we are cut from the same cloth as every other child. That our heart still beats. That pain still registers.

Failure is a skill like any other. Learning to be bad is practiced and it gets harder and harder to master the older we grow. Invisible Children never get to learn vulnerability. We do not know what it means to be incomplete. To admit to it. And to be loved still.

We disappear into young womanhood. Dehumanized by our competence. With no real idea of what struggling feels like, or for others to acknowledge our discomforts. We have no proof that we get love in spite of failure. Instead, we grow to assume perfect is the default. Help is never coming. We're holding our own hand in this life.

The ease of our way in the world is not hoped for. It is a given. When everyone around us reinforces and remarks on our ability, our sense of self displaces. Our worth is no longer within. We're bound to who we are outside. By what we do.

We grow up into the young women everyone watches and admires but that no one truly sees. *Competent* and *gifted* mask our flaws from the outside world. What is reflected back at us is that we are perfect. So we'd better be only perfect.

PERFECT PRESSURE

Perfect does not exist in nature. Perfect is not a human being. At some point, even the most gifted of Invisible Children meets her limitations. We come up against something we are not immediately good at.

If nightmares have a starting point, this is it.

I will never forget my first brush with shame. I was at my grandparents' house one evening after school. I was learning division. The sums did not make sense. I did not like the feeling, but the thought of saying, "I need help," felt like eating chalk. I had no idea how to form the words. I struggled for a while until I got some answers. I sat with my sweet little gran as she pored over my notebook to check my work. She nodded and said they looked good. I smiled and started getting excited about her lemon meringue pie. My favourite yellow treat.

The next day, I got my homework back. My teacher's brows were raised. Most of my sums were wrong. I could not look her in the eye. My cheeks flaming. A roiling heat zipped down my spine and my eyes pricked with tears. I quickly brushed my face with my grey cardigan sleeve to hide the evidence.

A few sums may feel like a small moment. It was not a small moment for a child who never got anything wrong. It felt like my world was collapsing into a black hole. A huge and horrible embarrassment. My heart imploding. *I wish my gran was dead.*

I vowed never to feel this way again. I decided to hate my gran for a year. I penciled her away. *Untrustworthy.*

PLUNDER

Imperfection is not a coded safety net for gifted children. Perfection is our mandatory tightrope. I had no idea what it felt like to be wrong in front of someone. With what felt like the world watching and expecting perfect, I committed to making imperfection invisible. To struggle silently.

And my brutal and destructive tool? Work. I learned how to work to the bone.

It is impossible to realise when an Invisible Child learns how to work silently. In the same way a cat will act her usual aloof self, then drop dead from kidney failure. The embarrassment of admitting, "I don't know the answer," after so many years of knowing everything is enough to seal a gifted girl's lips shut. The hot fear of getting another red X next to a long multiplication sum was enough to keep me in my room for thirty extra minutes until I could guarantee I was correct.

A mistake is not just a mistake. It is a referendum on our worth.

The silent working starts quietly. These small acts are the birth of internalized aggression towards the self. They precede suffering that, ten years later, hangs a Ghost Woman by the neck.

The rot sets in quickly. Even though my parents weren't forcing me to succeed, my whirring brain bypassed the innocence of childhood and turned everything into ruthless competition. Only one person could ever win. Perfect plundered joy. The ferocity I brought to play was infamous. Swiped board games littered floors, my face hot and angry, and my heart bursting with shame. It felt like my world ended every time.

So I stopped playing.

As I grew older and more reliant on victory to prove my worth, life turned into a game I could never win.

Fleeting moments of difficulty at a young age turn into the hours we spend in the gym chiseling our bodies into ironing boards. Flattening our breasts to the bone. I memorized entire science textbooks, including Tables of Contents, even though 90 percent of the book was not tested in exams. A faultless rendition of my times tables stood me in good stead for the hours I spent planning how little to eat.

For women like us it is One or it is Zero. Win or lose. Black or white. No in between. It was in my hooded heart, hunted by One, that perfect took root and became my weapon of choice.

BREAKING APART

Gifted children disappear in the moments where the external perception of what we are capable of sits at clear odds with the reality of our internal experience. There is a schism. A breaking apart. A fracturing of identity. Parents, teachers, siblings, and friends see what they've always seen. A child in her gift on a meteoric rise. In the absence of our honesty, they see a young girl as competent and capable as ever.

These tiny painful ruptures grow to cast long and dark shadows across a child's sense of self. The first fissures of self-doubt snake through our being. The first inkling that what is on the outside does not match our inside. The first whisperings of feeling like a fraud. It is in these moments where an Invisible Child learns how to weaponize her assumed ease. Foreshadowing a tolerance for struggle and work most people cannot begin to wrap their brains around.

Assumed competence is deeply destructive. When you are the only person who does not believe in you, rifts crack open. A burst lip. Two slabs of the Earth's crusts moving over each other, one slowly inching above and pushing the other down. Perception crushes reality. Assumed confidence shoves a fist in truth's mouth. It creates pressure that no human body should have to hold.

As the luster of being on top rusts in a torrent of internalized failure the stakes grow higher. How hard we have to work to stay effortless escalates. I will never forget the day I realised that in order to be me I had to exercise for at least four hours every day and hit an exact, miniscule calorie goal. *For the rest of my life.*

I saw time stretching out in front of me. So many years until I could rest forever. Dread hanging in the air. Cold and clammy and seeping through my pores. Pulling me down. It felt impossible. The unbearable burden of being me.

Maybe I just die now.

I could have questioned if this story was true. If I really had to live this way forever. I could have put my hand up. Except my hand was hammered to my side with an iron nail.

Ghost Women cannot ask for help. We are allergic to average advice. Questions undermine us. We have no voice to cry out. Would anyone listen if we did?

This unyielding and unspoken burden leads Ghost Woman

on a desperate hunt for ways to alleviate the pressure of being perfect. To soothe the fractures in our sense of self. To find ways to feel nothing at all.

We all have our breaking point. Even the perfect ones.

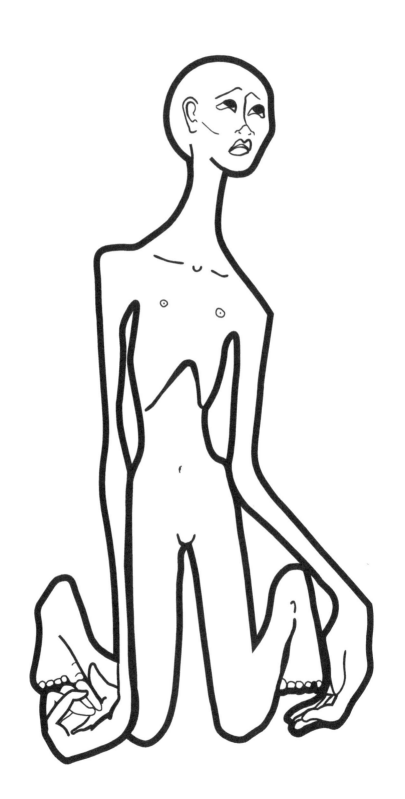

CHAPTER 2

Reckoning

WHEN PERFECT WOMEN BREAK

———

Years. The endless years. I would show up and do my thing. Dazzle. Or at the least, impress. And I'd go home and wish I was dead. I would starve. And then I would eat until I couldn't feel. And then unfortunately, I would wake up. And I would show up and do my thing. Dazzle. Or at the least, impress. And go home and wish I was dead. And I would starve. And then I would eat until I couldn't feel. And then unfortunately, I would wake up.

And I said it was fine.

Thirteen. Packed lunch is a nightmare. The food whispering in my rucksack. Sitting in the junior school bathrooms. The stink of industrial cleaner on me. My tiny tartan skirt and white shirt cutting into my waist. I rip open the plastic and shove the cheese sandwiches into my mouth, so fast I cut the roof. I don't stop as I taste blood. It's fine. I'm still the thinnest girl. Sixteen. I'm boiling a litre of water for breakfast. I pour sugar free juice into it. Hopefully, I won't be hungry until lunch. I tie my laces and run. Sometimes until I shit myself. It's fine. I'm the best on the team.

Eighteen. It's 5 o'clock in the morning. I wrap my finger around the hook and yank open the cold tinned herrings. I've been thinking about them since 3 o'clock in the morning. The stink of fish wafts through the room. I don't have a fork. The crunching of those tiny bones and slithery skin in my mouth feels good. I wolf them down like a stray dog. I tip the can up to drink the oil. Perhaps this will be my last meal of the day. It's fine. No friends left anyway.

Twenty. It's a New York summer. My skin sticky and warm in the darkness. My hands running all over my body. I love how successful my hip bones feel. My chest and stomach flat like a boy. It's hard to fall asleep hungry. It's fine. I'm going to be an All American.

Twenty-three. It's Monday and I wish I was dead. Again. Five days pretending to be human is hard to think about. My brain is laced thick with sugary sludgy pints of ice cream. I felt the same way last Monday. And the Monday before that. But it's fine. I'll work out harder today.

Twenty-six. My hand is in the bin. Now, I'm elbow deep rummaging. I saw my roommate scrape her pizza in here the other day. My knees on unwashed kitchen tiles. I can see where her teeth left marks in the cheese. Mould hits my nose. Just keep chewing. It's fine. Perhaps I'll fall asleep tonight.

Twenty-eight. I call in sick. Now I'm shopping. Three different stores so no one judges me. As if the guy paying minimum wage gives a fuck how much shit I buy. Ten o'clock in the morning, and I can feel my eyelids drooping. Passing out, half-eaten croissants, bags of crisps, pints of ice cream all around me. I wake up. The ice cream melted on my sheets. It's fine. I start my new life tomorrow.

It's fine.

It's fine.

It's fine.

Until it's not fine.

THE WRONG WAR

Ghost Women fight a long war. We believe with cold conviction that our greedy fat body is the demon we must face bravely, stiffen our resolve against, and banish to the hell she came from. Strip the bitch bare. Our body as the enemy is a convenient lie. It feels so real. The answer so obvious. How could there be any doubt that the reason we feel broken is because we cannot follow simple rules? *Shrink. That's it.* Controlling our impulses should be child's play for women like us. Except it's impossible. The reason it's impossible is simple.

The war you're fighting is not the war you think.

Think of all the times your hunger has overridden your ability to do anything. Saved you from the sickness of unspoken expectation. Maniacal lethargy. Tiredness so deep it quiets the chatter of your vicious mind, lulling you to sleep. Think of all the times hunger turned your body to stone. Binges dulling the vultures jabbing your brain, stalling with nausea. The warm relief of expecting nothing of yourself.

But to feel like hell.

The war you're fighting is not the war you think. Think of the years where you shrunk your body and forced people to pay attention to your dogged dedication. In shrinking, you also met the standards for our generation. The beauty of looking a little hungry.

Look at this body. Look at me work.

Starving for a tiny body is a powerful distraction from the burden of assumed ease. Eating yourself to stone is liberation from soul-crushing perfection. Brain swollen and slow like molasses, rocking the demon baby to sleep.

Shoving food down your throat until you puke is like the surgeon's knife slicing through a bulging cyst. Pent-up pain. A disgusting but delicious pressure release.

Exercising to the brink of injury and flat fatigue is the only way to rust the cogs of a mind that never stops connecting the ruthless dots that prove your worthlessness.

Food, or lack of it, is how the Ghost Woman copes. Over-working is another lifeline. What a testament to be fast and quick, *and* grind others into the dirt. We become slaves to our survival tactics. Riddling our body with so much stress and adrenaline that we are wired to the moon. Or dead on the floor.

This is the shadow side of perfect. The fight to feel visible or to feel nothing at all. The tactics we use to alleviate pressure end up manufacturing a huge amount of pain. The antidote becomes the virus. Our reckoning nears.

A NATURAL DISASTER

Ghost Women get so wrapped up in shrinking that we believe our body is our problem. We believe small will make us whole. But the heart of our suffering has nothing to do with food and our body.

We are lost in the loneliness of being the woman everyone assumes is fine. Remarkable. Resilient. We've never learned the lesson that no one expects us to be perfect. We live our whole fucking lives, stained with fear that we cannot be wrong, and loved still.

Fuck. Have we fought this war. Bravely. With the tools we know. We've carried a wand through life turning even the smallest and shittiest things gold. Silently cheating behind the scenes with invisible work.

We are so strong. But we are dead wrong.

Some things don't have to be perfect. But Ghost Women have no idea what that means. Our dogged lust for work and the deep shame of people realizing how ordinary we are keeps our hearts icy, our mouths shut, and our nose to the ground. Our pain tolerance is too high. Shoot us seven times through the heart, we find a way to rise up. Like a euthanized horse that refuses to die.

TURNING BLUE

Our body is a brain. Sensation is her language. Hunger is her asking nicely. Pain is her cry for help. As Ghost Woman, our body does not get a say. We pride ourselves on the override.

I was the queen of rising from the dead.

I treated my body so badly when I played field hockey at Syracuse University. It was the end of a successful season. We were fighting to win a national championship.

It happened during our second to last game. I jumped in the air to celebrate our winning goal and landed hard on the side of my foot. I fell flat on the ground. Wet plastic turf to the mouth. I didn't feel anything.

I tried to stand up. My ankle wobbled like melted chocolate. Pain scorching up my leg, my toes were spasming in my damp shoe. I screamed. My teammates hooked my armpits in their shoulders and walked me off the field.

Our physio sat me down and peeled off my long orange sock. My ankle looked like a fat grandma's. Pumped it up like a balloon, no bones in sight. Blood spread under the skin like an oil sick. The physio tried to hide her reaction. She failed.

Fuck my life.

I was rushed to the hospital for an emergency MRI.

"Can I play tomorrow?"

I choked it out through thick sobs.

The doctor shook his head. "You're done, kid."

"How long?"

"Twelve weeks of nothing."

The next morning I hobbled to the physio's room.

"Make it really tight."

She shook her head as she wrapped layers and layers of white tape around my ankle.

I could not feel a thing. The tape was so tight my shin skin hung over the edges. Bulging. Straining. My toes turning blue. Pins and needles. I could barely get my shoe on.

I played ninety minutes on one leg.

We lost.

As my teammates started picking up their equipment on the sideline, the trainer slung me over his shoulder and carried me off the field.

I sat by myself in the treatment room.

That's when it hit me.

Twelve weeks.

No running?

I'm going to get fat.

I binged that night.

I was in the gym the next day working out in a boot.

I didn't give a fuck how much my body hurt. I was her slumlord. She always paid.

THE BRINK

Your day will not look exactly like mine. But it will come. Something will happen to you. Or a collection of moments will add together deep inside and hurl you to the floor. You will realize the pain of being you is no longer a pain you can endure.

I wish it were different. But a Ghost Woman's pain tolerance has a deadly capacity. Your life may have to fall apart for you to finally pay attention to the right war. To that end, the pain of fighting your body will serve its purpose. Like a dangled carrot. Manufactured suffering gets you through the door.

You can lose weight one hundred times. When your core is rotten with shame, you will never shrink enough to escape yourself.

Hunger does not work forever. Small does not work forever. Work does not work forever.

All Ghost Women reach a tipping point when shrinking becomes symptomatic. Our attempts to lose weight intensify in their rigidity but stop working. Our binges grow more gut busting every time. I have heard so many stories about the day a woman's body yelled a forceful, "Fuck you." For one, it was almost shitting herself holding her daughter's hand in public. For others: emptying bank accounts and relying on parents to fund their primal hunger. Not speaking for three years. Skin mottling and breaking out in sores. Withdrawal from friendships. No light. No good in any world.

I felt many tremors when my body started shutting down. Eating food out of bins was a gentle one. Waking up wanting to die was not.

And no one saw anything. No one said a word. I never would

have stopped. But the pain got me in the end. Looking back. *Thank fuck.*

BROKEN

A Ghost Woman's pursuit of perfection is pointed and vicious. Our tolerance for suffering pushes us far beyond when a normal person would throw up their hands. I needed something to break my spine for me to stop.

That simple and profound wakeup call came when my body stopped responding to dieting. I started getting fat. Not fat in a way anyone else saw. Fat for me. My body ached with fatigue that no sleep could quell. A different injury every few weeks. And I was wracked with a torrid drive to eat. The hunger felt physical. Human. Bodily. A guttural scream. Like I had fifty ravenous lions living in my stomach desperate for meat and blood. I would eat like I was feeding a village of starving orphans.

I took a whole week off work to binge. I ate nearly 10,000 calories every day, slotted into the hours when I could guarantee I would be alone. My mouth bled as I crammed and choked on fistfuls of cheap cookies. Tubs of ice cream. Shoveled into my mouth then buried in the bottom of the bin. No amount of food would have been enough. *I need more.*

I could no longer stand my own torture. I began diets only to give up within hours. I would start fresh every morning at six o'clock when my alarm drilled through me. Reminding me of impending physical torture at the gym. I would sit up, only to smack a wall of fatigue. It bored down deeper than marrow. I would lie down, flattened by defeat.

Empty. So empty. I'd stare through myself in the mirror. Dead eyes. Nothing behind them. Barely human. Gone. I had to grab my wrists and squeeze them because I was not sure if my body was still there.

That's when I knew I was in trouble. In the same breath I felt bone-breaking, muscle-tearing, heart-ripping pain. I also felt nothing at all. When the scales started tipping and my restrictive periods could not mask the monstrous excess of my primal feasts, it felt like my world was ending.

When our bodies start fighting back, or breaking, we think we are in a lot of trouble. And we are. This is a good thing.

We've reached the brink.

Projecting pain onto the body is a ticking time bomb. It will explode. For Ghost Women, it needs to. We need to be brought to our knees because our tolerance for suffering is beyond human. It takes a natural disaster to flatten us on the floor.

In the animal kingdom, this is when the lioness starts walking out into the wilderness. She knows her time is up. She is no longer helpful, beautiful, or useful. She walks to nowhere until she falls down dead.

You are not dying. I won't let you. This bottoming out is your wake-up call. This is the moment when, for the first time, you can choose to tell the truth. After all these years.

This is the reckoning.

FALL APART WITH ME

I know you cannot break anywhere else. I know everywhere else you must be strong. But I can hold you. No thing you feel or say is too dark, too wrong, or too shameful. Let the pain rain on you. Fall apart with me.

All the times you grew up too fast. All the times no one saw you working. The times you took on what others could not hold. The burden of your brilliant mind that sees the patterns in ways others don't. The loneliness of vibrating on a plane not many know exist. All the times they cocked their head left or right, unsure how to respond to your quiet intensity. All the lost hugs you never knew how to ask for. Feel the weight of gifted press down on your chest. Fall apart with me.

Walk among the gravestones. Each one marks a day you abandoned your human heart. Again and again. All the ways being perfect cracked your spine with dirty boots. Feel the vertebrae crunching and swimming between your organs. And fall apart with me.

Take a thick black marker to all the events over the years you could not bear to attend. The swamping of your body in oversized clothes. The suffocating of the same body in hip-cracking tight jeans. The million times you made your body your battle cry. Fall apart with me.

Watch the fat bitches walking the streets. Pretending to be happy in all their folds of shame. Stare back at the dead eyes in the bathroom mirror. Fall apart with me.

Hear the ordinary people try to talk to you. Their boring lives rolling in front of them like a dumb mat. Watch them care enough to just scrape by. Envy how low their bar is. Fall apart with me.

Count every single rib, knowing there will never be enough. Pull at the fat on your body, feeling the shame and softness of excess. Fan the hungry flames of shame. Black out on a binge. Puke it out. Shit it out. Fall apart with me.

There will never be enough. Never enough hunger. Never enough smallness. Never enough cruelty and never enough admirating voices to lighten the doom that pulls you down to the pits of this black ocean.

That's the thing about pain no one sees. That's the thing about the pain and the fear and the struggle that never gets a voice, or acknowledgment, or honesty. Pain and us. We are one. We are committed to suffering because it gives us what we need. It shows us how fucked up we always knew we were from the moment our perfect spell broke. Even while the rest of the world stared, stupid and blinded by our fake brilliance.

Women like us. We are ruthlessly committed to feeling something. We are just as committed to feeling nothing. Down to the bowels of our being. Ghost Women think we deserve to suffer.

WAKE UP

You can stay here in the pits of your shame. You can walk out into the wilderness, lay down, fall asleep, and blindly hope tomorrow will be different. Or you can believe this crushing, oxygen-sucking emptiness is a message. That this pain has a purpose. That you can fall apart with me.

If you ever want to be free, I need you to wake up to the truth. You have fought the wrong war. Hard. And well. It has wracked your body like cancer. Torn you to bits and eaten your flesh. But this war with your body is a smoke screen. It's convenient. It's obvious. And it's a distraction. It's a distraction from the real work you need to do.

Shrinking masks the deeper pain. A hungry and broken body is nothing but the physical manifestation of a hurting heart. The sad yearning of a deadened soul.

Will you bury your head in the dirt, wake up, and continue to plunder? Or will you entertain the idea that a tiny body is not the only way to get the love you need?

Your own.

To answer that question, you must understand what shrinking gives you.

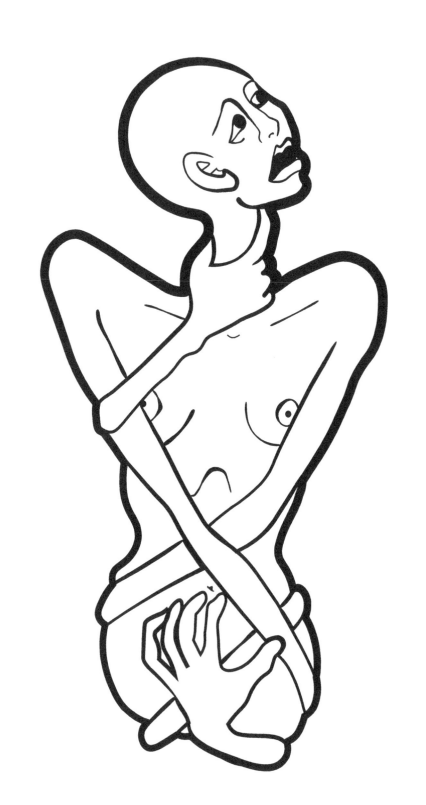

CHAPTER 3

Bone

WHY WE GO TO WAR WITH OUR BODY

———

A broken heart was always my favourite way to starve. Stuffed full of grief. It was just so easy to shrink.

Perhaps you know what I'm talking about.

I met him one night in my mid-twenties standing in a dimly lit bar. I thought he was blonde. When I woke up next to him the next morning his grey hair glittered. I stared at him for hours. Something in me knew he was different. Like I had found a whole new meaning for life.

Overnight.

I had the dream for a year before I had to shrink for his love.

I could not believe he had left me. It hurt me in ways I had never felt before. Perhaps the way a rabbit feels right before the hunter breaks its neck. Big fearful eyes, and then, crack, nothing.

Dying must feel like this.

I had imagined everything with him. And I was not a girl who grew up dreaming of a wedding. But he had me fooled. I allowed myself to fall.

Then he left me. He was gone. I knew I could make him see me again.

I started working. And by working, I mean starving.

Clues. There are always clues when our work is paying off. You know what I'm talking about.

Every body of every woman. We shrink differently.

But we make sure they see us working.

It works. Every single time.

I thin out from the top down. I see it in my face first. Hunger takes a saw to my thick round cheeks. Like the slow slicing of kebab meat. Sliver by sliver, down to the bone. I stand staring at myself in the bathroom mirror. The wiry hairs on my chin grow a little faster when I'm working hard. When I have more edges. I shave them off every morning so I can wear my hair up to the gym.

You could drown in the veins sticking through the skin of my forearms. Fat and blue raised river beds. My chest. Flat as a board. If I pull my shirt down I can see the tiny nub of my belly button. Normally nestled in a light blanket of tummy fat. Now stuck out like it did when I was 7. My bald cunt. Her lips

deflate, too. Tucked neatly away like a good and hungry girl.
Every month a celebration when I don't bleed. Thin enough to
dry me up. I can't spawn when I am starving.

It's a blessing. I never wanted kids. Except his. I wanted his.

At least every hour, a mirror check. The pursuit of thin. A ruler.
Even with no visible change, my tummy rumbling is enough.
Good. It's working.

It takes a while. Fat melts slowly, especially when your body
is already too hungry. Especially when it's the millionth time
you've done this.

It takes a couple of weeks for people to notice. But they do.

It took a couple of weeks for him to notice. But he did.

At least, that is what I believed. No thought that, perhaps, he
might love me in a way thin had nothing to do with.

My body talks to other bodies. Quietly whispering at first.

The smaller I get, the louder I roar.

Watch me. See me. See me work. See me rise. See my strength.
See me.

Heartbreak always worked a treat for me. Perhaps stress is
your petroleum. Or perhaps you're one of those women who
doesn't need anything more than the deep gurgling of pain to
keep your nose to the ground, your belly empty, and your eyes
on the prize.

To have your work witnessed is balm on deep wounds. Your efforts are seen. Your competence, your brilliance. Thin is the only acceptable way for people to see you work.

It's magic really. To bubble your pain to the surface. To use it to feed you so you don't need to eat a thing. While we fall apart and break inside, on the outside we have never looked stronger. They can't take their eyes off our hunger. All of them. Staring out from their ordinary skulls. Dumb eyes. And their small minds. And their lazy bodies. And their average lives.

We've never been more competent. We've never looked better.

I am never seen more than when I am small. My body of work. Borne witness. The applause.

They see you. They see me.

They come back to us.

Feeding on pain.

Shrinking to be visible.

It works.

It works every single time.

SHRINKING TO BE VISIBLE

Ghost Women turn to our body as the canvas to scream our invisible pain. In order to get noticed, we make ourselves small. By shrinking our bodies, we become more visible. The ideas seem at odds. But the smaller our body, the more space we take up. The more attention we get. The more real we feel.

We are experts at hiding how we struggle after so many years of brilliance. Ghost Women are scared of how the world will react to a bald and brave display of imperfection. Vulnerability is not a state of being we can embrace. But we cannot ask for help. Our weeping and roaring ego would never allow such treachery. We need endless reassurance that we are good. *Not good. The best.* The pressure has to be released somehow. We channel the pain and shrink the body.

Increasing our visibility by decreasing our physical size may seem counterintuitive. Until you remember the kind of world that we live in. The kind of world where the flow and undulation of a female body is shamed for her roundness and greedy, ugly excess. The small and lean body represents all that is applauded. *Work. Discipline.*

Ghost Women are not stupid. We know where the eyes go. By going to war with our bodies, we make our work visible in a way that ensures we are not weakened by the display. The opposite: we are strengthened. *Bold. Superior.*

Often, we do not starve to the point of bone-snapping frailty. Even in my smallest body, I did not look skinny sick. I danced the perfect line of small. Not so skinny that I looked vulnerable. Just lean enough that everyone could see my work and notice that I was different. Through my hungriest years you could see the vein topography scattering over my belly. I felt sick and high pushing on my fat veins as they rose up and pressed against my paper thin skin.

Ghost Women grow strong in our smallness. Lean and worked and purposeful. Our physical discipline adds to the gifts that are already assumed. By making our hard work physical, we are validated for our effort, when our achievements are otherwise assumed. The feeling is rare and precious. Why would we ever let it go?

SALLOW

I do not look like my brother and sister. It felt like the difference between sunbeams and rain. My easy-to-love siblings were blessed with my mum's genes; bigger foreheads, redder skin, lighter hair. Easy smiles.

I was small and dark. The sallow tinge of my dad's skin. Eyes that sunk easily. My difference did not end with looks. I would wake up at 6:09 in the morning every day without an alarm clock, shower for exactly seven minutes, do extra homework, eat a tiny breakfast with a teaspoon, and watch the news. I sat downstairs, clean, and combed, and ready, as my mum shook my siblings awake an hour or so later. Bleary eyed. Grumpy. Spooning normal amounts of cereal into their morning-breath mouths.

I was the black sheep. Eyes to the south as the rest of the flock faced north.

My fascination with being small and hungry started early. I was a picky eater. I had no interest in my bottle as a baby. As a small child, all I would eat for lunch was half a bread roll with butter and a carton of blackcurrant juice. I don't remember when the story that I was small started, but I heard it a lot growing up. It wasn't long before *small* wrapped its silky threads around my throat. By the time I was seven, I was weighing myself. I would stand on the green carpeted scales in the bathroom, count the numbers, and notice when they changed. Soon after that, I started standing in front of the mirror to practice sucking my tummy in.

I loved leaving food on my plate and hearing my mum telling her friends I just didn't have an appetite. I decided one summer I was allergic to chocolate. I sneezed a couple of times, made up a story, and then cut it out for nearly a decade. I started packing my lunches. A tiny cup of cottage cheese. Six tortellinis. No sauce.

I remember my first binge. It was around the age where being perfect had to be planned in advance. I remember eating a whole gallon of ice cream one night when my parents went out for a rare evening. The sugar licking my brain lulled me into a dumb stupor I had never felt before. It felt so fun to stuff myself. To eat in a way that was wrong. *Secretive. Bad. But good.*

Eating in secret became a game, but I realised that to earn the fun I needed to work to stay small.

A gallon of ice cream was child's play for the monster that grew to roar through me. Over the years, the binges grew wilder. The starving got hungrier. The compensation more violent. The lying thicker. The ends of the spectrum disappeared into opposing distances, pulling me apart.

INVISIBLE FIGHT

The choice to eat close to nothing or to overeat until we feel sick is not logical. There are smart and successful women all over the world who do one, if not both. At different phases in our lives, we may more actively pursue our smallness, or find ourselves stuffing to the brim.

Our suffering does not lie in weight alone: the lack or presence of it. It is the act of shrinking that tortures us. If you time-lapsed my body from ages fifteen to twenty-eight, you would not notice much of a difference. A couple of very skinny months in my early twenties. A fatter year after college. A few glorious lean, muscular, and tiny years in my mid-twenties when I practiced hunger and extreme exercise quite well. Day after day. Months. Years. A decade. Over and over, I would starve to the brink and then stuff my body full with all I could lay my hands on. Quieting my mind long enough to fall asleep and feel nothing.

To the world, nothing changed. I hid my body in baggy clothes to conceal the evidence. On the inside I shuttled between giddy hunger and crushing fullness. *Perfect. Monster.* Back and forth with every quarter pound gained and lost.

It felt like I was screaming underwater, dying for someone to notice how much I was hurting. At the same time, I did not want to be heard.

SHORN

There was no line I would not cross in some vain attempt to win my invisible war with weight.

I was eleven and fed up with being mistaken for a boy. I started growing my hair. For a few years, I combed it neatly into braids and tight buns. Every hair in place.

At some point, I let it go. It grew long and wild. Crawling and kicking down my back.

I always felt more myself without makeup. Now, my hair felt free, too.

And long hair was helpful. When my face felt fat, I'd pull the curls forward like a curtain over a half shut window.

One autumn in my mid-twenties, I found another convenient way to shrink: minimalism. I had thrown out most of my belongings and all my clothes. I boiled down my wardrobe to ten tops, two pairs of tight jeans, and enough pairs of black leggings for me to work out every day without doing laundry.

It felt good. *Superior.* My ode to needing very little of anything.

I was very lean. I even remember thinking I looked good. But the scale was not moving anymore. That was a problem.

I wanted to be my teenage weight again, and I was close. But so many years whittling away in gyms had left my body tiny and dense with muscle.

I looked in the mirror and saw the excess.

My hair. It had to go.

And a bonus! With no way to cover a fat face, I'd just have to stay thin. *Forever.*

The next day.

"All of it off. And black." The hairdresser looked at me, battle-worn from brave women who sit down in her chair and balk at the last minute.

"Are you sure?"

I was sure.

I felt calm as the curls fell.

Easy weight.

Sloughed off.

When I got home, I looked in the mirror. A short dark blind of black hair over pale winter skin.

It didn't look like me. I looked sick. Like Snape. I liked it.

I remember posting a photo of it. "Ten inches I did not need."

I stood on the scales the next day.

My weight was up.

I wanted to die.

What the actual fuck.

MAKING PAIN PHYSICAL

Fighting our body meets a grave need. The reasons why we go to war with our bodies are as simple as they are complex. Manipulating our bodies serves two very different masters, but both masters worship the same Holy Grail: The Ghost Woman's pursuit for visibility.

The first master Ghost Women bow to is acknowledgement. A small body is the way we hunt for the validation and support of others when the ease of our lives is otherwise assumed. In the eyes of those who watch us, our success is a given. They see our talents as the antidote to suffering. They think our gifts make us waterproof to the pain that rains on ordinary people. They watch us from a healthy distance and assume we do not have to work hard to feel good.

They cannot see how we die inside.

Shrinking our body is the only way Ghost Women feel safe displaying our pain in a form that strengthens, rather than weakens us. The control we exert over our bodies draws acknowledgement from mouths that otherwise say nothing.

I cannot tell you how many times I lay crying on the floor of a gym surrounded by spatterings of sweat, saliva, and blood. No shirt on, tiny shorts, and my visible abs thumping like a drum. Every single time I lay there wracked with pain, I got what I so desperately needed. A hearty slap of my hands. A shake of my shoulder. A kind and strong voice validating how impressive I was. Warmed by admiration, with the tiniest undercurrent of envy. Sometimes, I would stagger to stand, someone would offer their body, and I would lean into it, hungry for the fleeting chance to accept help. Resting on their body felt like crack. In these appropriate displays of pain, I have never felt more human. More loved. More seen.

For all my gifts, I was not born beautiful. I was not the girl men or women drooled over. But I was stopped on city streets throughout my twenties because of my body. Women admiring my flat stomach and cute ass. Athletic men acknowledging my leanness. They knew how hard it was for a woman to look like this. *How do you do it?*

In all other realms of my life, I shut my mouth. I made it known I worked out twice a day. I used scales to weigh my salad in the office kitchen. Five tiny pieces of chicken. I took a measuring cup on my mid-afternoon walk to make sure the black iced coffee I bought had exactly ninety calories of cream in it. A two-hour training session and five miles commuting on my bike filled the hours between. A protein bar for dinner.

Never not exhausted. Never not wearing something tight and black. And unlike everything else I did, my fight did not go unnoticed. After so many years of invisible struggle, everyone started asking me if it was hard to endure. To abstain. To suffer. *Finally. You took for fucking time.*

It was like water on a thirsty tongue. With my heart leaping, and eyes glinting, I got to acknowledge that yes.

Yes, it is fucking hard work to be me.

I suffer and work, too, you know. In a remarkable and noble way. *Unlike you.*

The diets, the work, and the engineering of the body are an acceptable way for Ghost Women to whisper our humanness. When we express pain physically, we grow ever more exotic to those who lack the fire of fear. A unicorn. *Special tastes so good.*

They see what they see. We get what we get. At long last. Someone asking us how we are. How we do it. If we are okay. Bowing at our feet. Validation of perfect work.

STALK

When you are a Ghost Woman, you see other Ghost Women everywhere. Like black light cast on a crime scene. Late night at the office. On the running paths. Certain aisles at the grocery store. Turning over food packets and scanning labels. You see them sitting in restaurants at the weekends gorging on burgers and macaroni and cheese. "I earned this." Shame and fear dulling every bite, knowing it's back to poverty rations tomorrow.

I would stalk them in the locker room at my gym, catching glimpses of their partly naked bodies in angled mirrors. We would pay lip service to each other's efforts while wishing each other dead. Hot fury when they got the attention I wanted. Stabbing them in the back the minute they walked out of the room. That is how ruthless I was.

That is how ruthless our need for acknowledgement is. When we are fighting for our visibility, every other Ghost threatens our spotlight. Their success only spurs us on to shrink more.

NUMBING TO SURVIVE

The second master the Ghost Woman bows to is the curation, or numbing, of pain. Perfect has wrapped and calcified
around us. Squeezing. Strangling. The work required to
maintain the mirage is painful. But the fear of being discovered as a fraud is excruciating. We cannot entertain it, even
for a second.

There are only so many hours in the day. Being perfect takes
all of them. It eats time alive. The pressure building inside
feels like colliding magma deep in the heart of the Earth.

The centre cannot hold. The pain must be expressed.

For Ghost Women, we deal with pain through two channels.
One, we blow the face off a volcano and binge until we feel
nothing. Or two, we redirect the pain towards our body and
feed on it, instead of food. Many Ghost Women use both
weapons. An endless cycle of a few sickening days of feasting,
followed by weeks of famine.

I felt most relaxed, and therefore weak, around food when
I was in love. Fun dates at restaurants and ice cream at
theirs after. Once I found myself back home, and alone, fear
slammed down and Sunday evenings turned into monster
binges. *You've fucked up, so why not fuck it all the way up?* I'd
pass out dreading the dawn. Another sweat-drenched hungry
Monday beckoned.

Love was greedy. But heartbreak? When love and happiness
were gone? I could eat despair for weeks and starve with ease.
And I learned the tactic young.

FLAKY MOUSE

I was fifteen. He was older than me. It was the first time I had ever been in love. He felt like a man to me. Big and broad shoulders. Sandy hair. A touch of ginger. And this goofy smile. So quick to light up his whole face.

He had nearly died the year before from meningitis. They cut the tumour out of him. A tangerine-sized lump of death. Surgery left a massive scar wrapping around the side of his neck. I would run my fingers over it. It felt brave.

We met up in Glasgow's city centre on Saturdays and would take the bus to his place. His mum was open, and friendly. She didn't mind that the door was closed.

I had never felt anything like it. I would spend twenty minutes crafting perfect text messages on my old brick mobile phone. Strict character limits made for profound love haikus.

It was the perfect six months. Then suddenly he broke up with me. I remember leaning against a wall in the corridor outside the school gym. The gruff bricks scraping my back. Him standing opposite me. Eyes down.

The gym was my arena. Where I always won.

Not today. *Fucking loser.*

I'd known about her. He'd told me she was his best friend when we first met. Within weeks, they were dating. A mousy girl with peeling skin in the year above me. She was dull. A washed-out dish towel. Blotchy. Her voice was small and wimpy like an ugly rabbit.

He chose her.

I had never felt anything like it before.

I felt naked, broken, and out in the open. Cast off. It was a public and personal failure. I did not know how to speak.

I could not talk without choking on tears. Every word felt like an admission.

I started screaming the only way I knew how. I stopped eating.

It worked. I screamed invisibly. In time, I forgot about him.

Twelve years later, I was in real love. A man with grey hair, not a boy pretending. So many years between. So many hungry and full years of silently screaming my pain. He left me, too.

And when he did, I starved with a quiet tunnel vision that, looking back, scares me as much as it impresses me. The tightness of the fixation. The latching and the feeding on pain.

I could not forget this love.

This time, there was no mouse.

Starving worked.

Or, perhaps, he actually loved me.

I didn't care.

All I know is he came back.

Love.

It always brought out the best of the worst of me.

LIABILITY

Ghost Women are desperate to feel something. We are also desperate to feel nothing at all and the body is the perfect tool to get both. Our hunt for visibility or numbness gets more extreme with time. When I was eighteen, I would run every day for an hour. By the time I graduated from playing Division 1 hockey, four hours was the norm. I peaked at twenty-seven. Every day, and every night, I crushed my body at the gym. I ran fast to the point of puking. I swung on bars until my hands bled. I wept on the floor. I hired an online coach to remind me that the calories in gum count. Anything to help me minimise. I'd finally lie down at night. Dead to the work for a few sweet hours.

Using the body for significance is intoxicating for Ghost Woman. We strive for straight and emotionless. We seek to control and manipulate variables. The method is logical and structured. But in straightening out our bodies with ruthless efficiency, we strangle the gift of flow.

Polarity exists in all humans. We all have a natural pull: the ability to receive from others and nurture. We all have a natural push: the linear qualities of organization and rational thinking. Ghost Women live in a society built on force and work within a larger ecosystem of fat shaming and thin privilege. We have no evidence that we get what we need without working because our gifts gaslighted us at birth. Help is not coming. Trust is a liability. We would not know how to receive support if we tried because it codes in our system as lazy. *Pathetic. Girly.*

Trust is not cute. It is the danger zone.

Ghost Women abort our pulling energy young and learn to only push. We abandon all semblance of balance. Our pushing energy is drunk on our fear of failure so we fall into distortion. We make ourselves dark and harsh and emotionless. We bow to the numbers and screw the nature.

THE LIMIT

Ghost Women spend years acting like we want our body dead in hopes that one day we will earn a life worth living. Over time, our body transforms into a physical manifestation of our emotional fractures. A war crime against the self.

I lost my period for nearly a decade. I grew facial hair all over my chin and lip. In the space of two years, I broke my face and my wrist, and I tore my knee to bits. I rehabbed all my injuries like a fiend. I was overpowered by the fear of how to feel real if I couldn't shrink.

Waging war against the body is a campaign to feel real. To feel human. But we grow infuriated by the limitations of our physical body. We reach target weights, only to shift our goal posts. We have finite fat to melt and shrinking is exhausting. The lies we tell ourselves about a certain weight guaranteeing happiness grow harder and harder to believe. We start aching on a cellular level.

It gets harder and harder to scrape excess off our bones. What used to fall off quickly sticks stubbornly like glue. Our bodies, wracked with distrust and stuck deep in survival mode, beg us for rations. Hunger is no longer a gentle chorus but a dissenting scream.

The moments after I finished a meal were terrifying. The plate of Brussels sprouts and turkey did nothing to quiet the roar. I would stare at the clock knowing it was a full three hours before I was allowed to eat rice cakes dipped in protein powder.

Smallness gives us purpose. It gives us hope. But the mental pressure of restriction is exhausting. The constant battle against our hunger takes inhuman strength. At a certain point, our bodies cannot take the abuse any longer. Like an addict who can't find a vein. There is no more space on the body's canvas to scream. *Now what?*

The pressure to be perfect is a weapon. We did not write the storyline alone.

CHAPTER 4

Spider

OUR IDENTITY IS A WEB OF UNTRUTHS

———

My grandpa would stand outside the school my parents couldn't afford waiting for the bell to ring. He looked like an ancient tree creaking in a rotting forest. Twinkling eyes. Kind smile. So old. Massive crab hands. Bark thin enough to see the rivers of bloody sap keeping him alive.

So many circles around the sun.

The bell would ring. He would look down and there I was, standing silently beside him. Five years old. Barely reaching his knee cap. Shorn dark hair, and a rather unfriendly look on my face. I doubt I said hello.

He loved me. I loved him. I knew he wanted to hold my hand. But I couldn't do it. I didn't hold any hands. Let alone crabs' hands.

He would stand there looking down at me. A sigh dropping out of him. Defeated.

"Such a Contrary Mary."

That's when he would place his hand at the base of my neck. And walk me across the busy road.

I guess this is what dogs feel like.

I was a mystery to him. Oblique. Hiding away in corners as my brother and sister beamed and smiled in open space.

He always saw me as the opposite.

He loved me. He did not understand me.

There were children.

Then there was me.

Contrary Mary wasn't meant to be cruel. For a long time, I thought it was cute. But the story slowly wrapped its silk around me over years. Over decades. I heard it crawl out of so many mouths. Parents. Sister.

A way for others to understand me. A way to hold me neatly in their hands.

Eyes rolling to the sky. There she goes again.

And I was complicit. I found a million reasons why I was Mary.

Twenty years passed.

He was just shy of one hundred when death felled him.

I missed my grandpa's funeral because I was on a diet.

I loved my grandpa.

But I needed to be thin by July.

His death was inconvenient.

So I did not go.

What kind of person does that?

Contrary Mary does.

THE IDENTITY WEB

Identity is a cold comfort. It is our imperfect way to cast structure around something that is impossible to ever understand. The slippery, formless, and undulating magic of the human spirit. When we use words to describe a human being, it is impossible to be correct. We do our best, through the slanted lens of our own experience. We wrap everyone we meet up in slivers and story threads. We bundle them up into a neat package. *This is who you are.* As young children, our identity is created by stories spun about us, long before we have a voice of dissent. A Ghost Woman's childhood hangs a noose around her neck.

We are raised by spiders. We are held in imperfect hands. We grow up on bread crusts and butter, and the stories that our family, and chosen family, and perfect strangers spin about us. The silky threads of stories created my identity. Our identity. In the moments I turned my tiny cheek to the left and refused to suck the bottle. *She's not an eater.* In the moments I stumbled across the kitchen floor at eight months old, dumbfounding my mum because my brother walked at fifteen months. *She's a quick one.* In the moments my sweet grandpa muttered 'Contrary Mary.' *She's a little dark and twisty.*

Identity is not just narrated. It is reflected back into our wide eyes. I saw the way people looked at me. Talked about me. I felt the envy dripping off the girls in my class when I won. *Again.* I felt how teachers got stuck in the gravitational pull of my strange moon. Their eyes grew glittery and kind as I recited a sixteen-page poem about dinosaurs I learned by heart for no reason.

Good girl. Smart girl. Perfect girl. Small girl. I grew up basking in warm compliments, and my endless achievements reflected and validated the praise. Poetry, music, sport. I stood up and won. I always found myself in the middle of the front row of photos. Sitting neatly, holding a trophy, or playing the starring role in the nursery rendition of *The Three Little Pigs*.

They all said it. I heard it. And it felt true. Perfect was in my blood.

I wrote all my homework with the tiniest handwriting I possibly could. Only those who really looked deserved to read what I wrote. I sat quiet and well-behaved in the car seat as my mum yelled at my older brother for punching me. Not only perfect but perfectly behaved. An avid avoider of crossed words. Who I was felt special.

But perfect is not an identity. It is a death wish.

If only someone had told me that story.

Our identity forms in the moments where we hear or see what others tell us is true. Your stories may be different from mine, but all Invisible Children disappear.

We don't get a say in who we are. Before we've even learned to talk, the stories are spinning. The hooks dip and sink into our souls. The web adds another thread; day after day, the silk knits together. Whoever we are becomes more concrete and undeniable, cocooning us inside something that, one day, we identify as the person that we are. The woman that we have to be. No matter the cost.

Parents are spiders. They spin like no other. Some are evil, and tricky, and guilty. Mine were not, the opposite. Often they seemed embarrassed by how often someone made it clear I was good. I was also the child who was difficult to quantify and grapple with. When everyone else was facing left, I was facing right. I was not always the easiest to love. Everything that made me brilliant made me prickly to touch, a heady mix for creating emotional distance.

Iona is the name of a tiny beautiful island off the west coast of Scotland. My dad's parents told my mum and dad it was a ridiculous choice. They were wrong. Iona was the perfect name for a Ghost Woman. A thin spidery tendril. Not a name you forgot. Never two in a class. Often mispronounced but admired. "That's a beautiful name." Always a follow-up question. Especially when I moved to America.

I loved it. Noteworthy from the day I was born. *Special.*

I was born a tiny island.

Admired from a distance but rarely visited.

And not because people did not love me. No one who said I was perfect meant to be cruel. But in making me faultless, they cast me adrift. Off shore was a mutual and comfortable distance.

My parents tried to understand their tiny island, but they had lost the map, or never had one in the first place.

All Ghost Women are islands. An Invisible Child's experience is different from a child who grows up unremarkable. We stand blinking in the spotlight. Quietly beating a tragic drum. We get the eyes and we get the glory but the experience is a lonely one because no one knows how to share the joy with us. We don't know how to grab and squeeze their hand either.

So they watch. And they listen. But they don't see us. How early, and urgently, and effortlessly we shine drives us further away from those who care. Everywhere we go, a small but magical little stranger. Turning mud to gold.

People think we don't need them. People think we don't like them, so they weave stories to box us off. To mitigate our prickles. The stories centre on our gifts and talents, squared and amplified by our willful independence.

And the threads. They thicken.

Good girl. Smart girl. Perfect girl. Small girl. Leave her alone.

We float away. Ever alone.

A silky noose around our neck.

THE END OF LOVE

What happens when an Invisible Child gets hints that she is not perfect? I will never forget the humiliation of practicing my handwriting, making a mistake, trying to erase it, ripping the paper, and crying when my teacher told me off. I will never forget the day a gymnastics teacher tutted and said I didn't "have the splits in me." I will never forget when I placed second in a throwing competition. I will never forget smashing a tiny ornament in a gift shop by accident. Rosy red embarrassment burning up my mum's cheeks as she whisked me out the door.

Invisible Children have never learned how to be wrong, and these moments scar us. We think they mark the end of love. Like a bullet straight through the heart. As we confront struggle for the first time, our identity does not swell to house our humanity. The silky threads do not loosen to accommodate the truth that we are not perfect.

Instead, the threads tighten around our throats and shut us up. And no one notices because our competence has kept the world distanced. In our audience, clapping and admiring our show. When a smart child is confronted by her own limitations, she faces an impossible choice. To submit to imperfection, or to start working a little harder. When you grow up believing to the core that perfect is what you need, that special is who you are, there is no choice.

A story repeated often enough becomes true. In the moments where we choose to be perfect over telling the truth and learning how to be wrong, or bad, the story threads and our biological blueprint fuse together. We make a choice. We assume the identity that has been created for us. We turn black, and beady-eyed. Backed into corners that start to feel like home.

Powerless yet powerful. We start to spin with wild abandon, weaving our ghostly identity together.

CASTING SHADOWS

We think we need to breathe to survive. And we do. But the most gut-thirsty oxygen sucker is not our physical body. That honour goes to the threads that construct our identity. Like a screaming baby, the stories that wrap our souls in lies need constant feeding.

Invisible Children learn how others see us, and the pressure of expectation drives us forwards. When our parents, teachers, and everyone else we deem important is still acting as if we are the second coming of Einstein, who are we to raise a hand? I heard over and over again I was special. *Black sheep. Lone wolf. A once-in-a-lifetime kind of girl.* What choice did I have but to gather breadcrumbs to prove the truth?

What choice did you have?

When *perfect* wraps its tendrils around our neck, we learn to quietly and silently work. We take on the mantle the spiders created as they watched our DNA play easily and effortlessly with life. This conscious choice to conceal struggle, save face, and dazzle endlessly foreshadows our impending emotional torture.

In these moments, we disappear. No human is home ever again. We pull on the mask and start acting out the role we are destined to play. We start to work hard when no one knows we're working. The hidden work starts small. The lies start small. Our suffering starts small. But in ten years, the schism between external perception and internal reality manifests as a fully blown fraud complex.

STICKY

"Does he hurt you?"

The nurse looked at me. Worried.

My arms were covered in messy scratches. Soft light purple bruises. Fading to an ugly green.

I was torn up from lifting concrete stones at the gym that morning.

I could still hear the echoes of awe as people watched me work.

I laughed. She thought I was being abused.

And I was. But not by a man.

I was getting impatient.

Is this what it's like trying to get birth control in America?

She shot it into my arm. A thin black rod. It sat just below my bicep.

I loved it. Slow steady hormones dripping through me every month without having to remember pills. Not that I had a period anyway.

I came back three years later so they could remove it and put in a new one.

The same room.

I rolled up my sleeve.

"This will be quick."

She started softly digging into the skin. A few minutes passed. Ten minutes. Twenty.

She was ruffled.

She left the room and came back with new, more urgent tools.

"It's really stuck."

"It's because you're so lean."

"I've never seen an arm like this on a woman before."

My heart jumped.

Special. Hard working. Unusual.

I could barely contain my glee.

She kept jabbing and trying to twist.

I didn't even mind the pain.

It felt so good.

This dark little pocket in my arm.

Stuck to me. A reflection of all I was. All my work.

"It doesn't want to let go. It's like it's part of you now."

Damn fucking right it's part of me.

The leanness. The pain. The tiny body. Latched on and wrapped round. Embedded. Embodied.

Story webs grow sticky as they age. They melt and mould into us. We drop strands through air. Morning dew speckling the web. It gets easier and easier to stick out our tongues and catch the flies.

CASTING SPELLS

As we grow up into Ghost Women, we fully assume the role of the spider. The stories depend on us. Our lives depend on them. Our dark independence stops people from landing on our island and the distance protects us. They do not see or feel how fast our feet paddle below the surface to keep our island afloat.

We are caught in the cast spell. We are puppeted by the silky story slivers. We do all we can to maintain the mirage. No matter the cost. No matter the pain. No matter the stirring fear or the dull and achy sadness.

Like the barrel of a gun.

We stare down years of harder and faster and more brutal invisible suffering.

The surrendering of *perfect* is a fate worse than death. It cannot ever come to pass. We are enmeshed in the lies, and our pain tolerance is high. We cannot imagine a world where we are not held in the highest regard.

There are standards. And then there are Ghost Women standards. In Scotland, anything above 70 percent is an A. I had a 97 percent rule. Anything less meant I was vulnerable to not being on top. I craved the head nod from my teacher, as much as I craved the look of hatred on the boy's face I always inched out. Like a drug. I needed it, running to the bulletin board at the end of the year to see my name next to every single class prize available. The cementing of myself.

There she goes again. *What can't she do?*

There was only one correct answer.

Nothing.

It did not matter that by the end of every school term my mouth was littered with angry and painful ulcers. I'd suck on salt and vinegar crisps to make it worse. Thick and murky mucus lodged in my throat, my nose raw from colds that lasted months. I endured sickness that left ordinary children at home. Where they should be.

And I was perfect. I did not miss a day of school in fifteen years.

I never learned how to admit defeat. Sport was torturous. I could never just win. I had to win well. I would sit and stew, scream at myself silently, and then swallow the shame whenever I did not play as well as I wanted. Fixating on one bad pass.

I never learned how to sink into my mum's body and weep with disappointment when I lost the odd tennis match. I was so used to her loving me from a distance I did not think hugs were part of her mothering. Until I watched her hold my distraught little sister with such tenderness that thick flames of fury blackened my lungs.

I remember watching a college teammate sitting in her dad's lap after a bad loss at field hockey. She was smiling through crusted tears. I remember wondering if she could feel his penis underneath her. Pressing against her. I blinked. I realised I was staring. I could not take my eyes off them. My face slack. Mouth gaping. The closeness felt sick. The vulnerability made me ill.

PLAGIARISM

The Invisible Child. The Ghost Woman. We are watched. We are never truly seen. The flashing of the underbelly. The lifting of the veil. We cannot have it. And we need it that way to keep the stories alive. We plagiarize our life by stealing what others think is true.

Stealing is wrong.

But is it really stealing when we *are* the lie?

All Ghost Women reach a tipping point where we make deception our life's work. The separation between the spun story and our sense of self collapses. And that's when we are in a lot of trouble. When the stories get fed up with our skin and bones they start eating through our souls like worms through a rotten apple. The stories stifle our souls and become more true than who we are. The embodied lies suffocate us.

The shadow cast by a spider's story is as hungry as it is long. It is lonely working in darkness, pumping lifeblood into the ways we believe others must witness us. Working so hard to ensure no one finds out our secret.

We are complicit. We cannot stop. Our humanity disappears in childhood, and we never get it back. We abandoned the chance for honesty a long time ago. We are rendered invisible by the stories slipping casually from other people's mouths and then choked out of our own.

At first, we were caught in someone else's web.

But now?

We are the spiders.

Our silk. Our lies. Our throats. Hung by a million threads of our own making.

And the spider is getting hungrier, but do not fear. You are a hunter trained in hell.

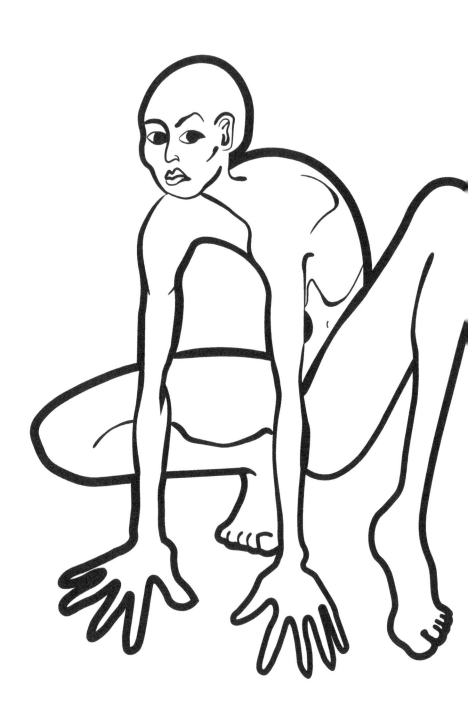

CHAPTER 5

Wolf

WE FEAR BEING DISCOVERED A FRAUD

———

We startle awake. Begging silently for mercy. Please, not today.

She's already here.

Hot stale breath warming cool dawn air. Her claws digging into your stomach. Her tail wrapping around your throat. Her cold clammy scales covering you in a thin film of doom. Her fangs bared. Her beak drilling into rich fatty marrow. Nothing more delicious on her tongue than the taste of her own fear.

It's not like she should be hungry. She feasted yesterday. And the day before that. And the years before that, too.

A bottomless stomach. A reckless need to plug these gaping holes.

Hunting the self.

It does not exist in nature. There is a hierarchy to the kingdom. An order of dominance. Animals hunt and they kill each other. They feast on the flesh of the weak and are someone else's lunch.

They succumb to the order. The birds sing. The rivers gurgle. Grass grows. All is well.

Not here. Not us.

There is nowhere to hide when the one you fear the most sleeps in the same body. When you are the whole food chain. An ecosystem of one. No natural predator.

The hunter.

The hunted.

And every day she awakens a little hungrier. Her demands a little louder. Her fear a little more urgent.

Prove yourself. Tend to my wounds. Feed my stomach.

So you can rest your head. Go ahead. Sleep.

I'll see you in the morning.

When you wake up, you better be running.

BONE FROM BONE

Feeling like a fraud is a deep and complex experience. There was a time in history when people who committed treacherous acts were killed by stretching. They were tied on boards, hands and feet nailed down. Then their bodies were pulled apart.

Ghost Women lie on the same boards. We hammer our own nails. The ripping apart of the self is something we know well. The contrast between how we are perceived and how we feel inside tears us bone from bone. Our perfection rips and strains against the power of crushing self-loathing. No wonder we feel like frauds. We live our lives terrified others will realise how ordinary we are. We are even more terrified to face ourselves. To witness our own flabby humanity. Our shortcomings. The vulnerable spots where we are average. We are ruthless defenders of our own fear. We are both the hunter and the hunted.

POLAR

Ghost Women live in a paradox. If we only felt one way about ourselves, life would be quite simple. At least we would know we were special. At least we would know we were worthless. Without doubt. Without question. But that is rarely true for women like us. It is not just the way we feel about ourselves that is different from the way others experience us. It is not as simple as thinking we are not good enough, while others think we are extraordinary. We also believe we are extraordinary.

We believe to the bone we are special.

Our deep fear of being discovered a fraud is fought by a

jubilant and healthy knowing that we are very gifted. Our aching need to lie down and rest for a moment is countered by awareness of just what we are capable of.

More. We are capable of so much more than the average person. We get sick joy using ourselves as a measuring stick to comment on how pathetic everyone else is. Our bodies are also wracked with terror that the same people we sneer at will catch us in a blind spot and see we are just as worthless as they are. The polarity pulls us to pieces.

It is normal for Ghost Women to think we are better than everyone else while feeling like shit on a shoe. It is normal to feel smug at how slow other people are while wishing our lives were simple like theirs. It is normal to only care about our own happiness and a moment later shame our needs. It is normal to suffer hard to get attention then hate ourselves for being so desperate. It is normal to stand awe struck that no one has noticed our radiance and then question if we deserve to eat lunch.

In any given moment, Ghost Women shuttle from confident motherfucker to quivering wreck and back again. Constant contradiction. Constant conflict. We sit at the phantom door waiting for everyone to bang on it and yell, "Fraud!" through the keyhole. These contradictions are the nails in our palms and feet that stretch us to our breaking point.

PUMBAA

I had the grades to do anything. I chose to paint. I studied for a year in Scotland before I moved to America. The art school was famous. A little gem nestled in my hometown.

I thought I was the one with wild ideas. Here, I was dish water.

How could I compete with a student who videoed himself shaving his pubic hair, placed it in a jar, burned it, and called it a painting?

It was the first week of class and the theme was Phenomenology. The philosophical study of the structures of experience and consciousness. I drew a piece of crumpled paper. *Deep.*

I made two friends in the first week. They looked like Timon and Pumbaa.

He was thin. Painfully thin. Like a bird. I felt my eyes running all over his tiny body. Like I was eating it. The knobbles of his knees sticking through perfect rips in tight black jeans. His mouth. Flanked by big lips. The quiet lilting beauty of the Scottish highland accent flowing and wrapping around me as he spoke. He laughed at my jokes. All the gays do. I liked him immediately.

She stood next to him. Like a nightmare. This massive bulbous body. Like a big blow-up bouncy ball stuck on spindly sticks. A tick. Fat and full of blood. She was loud. *So loud.* Yelling about dunking chocolate biscuits in milky tea and bad television.

I hated her art. She drew hideous and messy sketches of poor people from parts of Glasgow I had never visited and stuck them haphazardly on the wall with so much tape.

Not neat. Not art. She was foul.

Somehow, she had one million friends. I would watch her eating whatever she wanted and drinking white Russians like mother's milk.

She took up so much space in rooms she made me sick. And she would not leave me alone. She kept saying it in front of other people:

"Come out with us."

"Have a drink!"

"Have fun."

"Lighten up!"

Fuck off, you fucking bitch.

I couldn't. Not now. Not ever. Her fun did not feel safe. It felt fat and carefree and wrong and it did not fit in with the woman I was allowed to be.

I feared she was hunting me. Seeing everything. Seeing how fucked up I was behind my neat little drawings.

I tried to squash her like a bug.

I started ignoring her completely. Giving her the ice shoulder. I talked quietly about her and her stupid messy drawings. But I was out of luck. No one fell at my feet in art school.

It was a new feeling for me. Average. Not interesting. No one cared that I was in the studio at eight o'clock in the morning or that I worked out for hours every day. They cared if I got fucked up with them at the piss-stained college bar. I was surrounded by wild young people taking horse tranquilizers, not showing up for months at a time, not caring about grades, and having a good time.

Perfect didn't really work here. It was uncomfortable at first, but it quickly became torture. After a year, I could not take it anymore. I dropped out. Two months later, I moved to America.

I thought I would feel free. *A new country. A new me.*

But pain has a passport.

Suffering was on my tail.

ECHO CHAMBER

A Ghost Woman's fraud complex does not whisper quietly. It screams. We are expert navel gazers. We believe that everyone is watching us and waiting for us to fail. People we have met once. People who don't know or care about us. Strangers. The fear of others seeing through our act breathes down our necks like a stinking beast.

I was so scared of other people seeing through my act that there was nothing I would not do, and no person I would not walk on, to make sure I looked strong. I slaughtered a hundred more Pumbaas before I realised I was the wolf hunting myself.

It is convenient to make everyone else the arbiters of our

fate. To make how they see us important. Perhaps they are watching. Perhaps we do feel their eyes sometimes. Perhaps we are worthy of note, or a conversation. But in reality, they do not give a fuck about us. Not in the way we think they do. The vicious hunter stalking for prey is us. The Ghost Woman. Lusting for our own blood. The audience we fear so much is an externalization of our internal wolf. A hate-fueled projection.

Ghost Women are masterful self-stalkers. The hunting of the self is circular. There is no natural end point. Our skull is an echo chamber of fear. The hunted parts of us quiver in corners, as the hunting parts of us wait to pounce and feed. Like sniffer dogs gnashing teeth through our own guts.

The wolf gets hungrier, and our definition of perfect grows more belligerent and demanding. We hunt ourselves in darker and colder and more ruthless ways.

We run. But deep down we know. We're not getting out alive.

THE OUTSIDE SELF

Ghost Women are exhausted by the work it takes to maintain our illusions. We are also married to the game. Fear is a cold mistress, and an endless burning ember, and there is good reason for Ghost Women to suffer. Being a ruthless hunter of the self does not go unrewarded.

Our world rewards wolves.

Who cares if we live in a nightmare? Fear is fraud's running mate: a powerful creator. She makes us magnificent. Fear got me what most people can only dream about. I represented my country. I was a Division I All American. I graduated with a 3.98 GPA. A man I met once gave me nearly £30,000 to help me go to graduate school. A single wire transfer. "You're special. It's clear." A company paid thousands for my green card even though I had no formal training for the job position. I squatted double my body weight and ate cold hard-boiled eggs for lunch most days to make sure I looked good doing it.

Hunting was painful. But I got everything I wanted. In all of our darkness, we shine so brightly. The glory makes it hard to ever want to stop.

The wolf we're running from lives inside us. We hopelessly act out the gifted child prophecy to keep the applause loud, our throat above water, and our bellies fed for the night. The buoyancy keeps the demons quiet, in moments. But at no point are we happy. We can never truly win. At no point can we rest. When our worth is dependent on output, we fear for our lives if we stand still.

We are hunted by the fear of who we are standing still. We commit over and over again to living our lives on the run in constant pursuit of money, an award, or a small enough number on the scale to arrive at a destination that does not exist.

We may dream of resting our head. Living in a quiet place where we are enough. Days off. Leaving it all behind, traveling, or working on something we really care about. *In our dreams.* Ghost Women have no idea what we care about. We work too hard at everything to know what we like.

Perfect always trumped enjoyment. So rest never comes. The

dreams are well-dressed lies. If we let them feel true for a moment too long, the wolf breathes fresh fear through our blood.

We can't only be good at some things. Ordinary is not an option. This mirror cannot crack. The spell cannot be broken.

Ghost Women know in our hearts that if we want to survive, we cannot stop running. We know in our hearts that tomorrow we will wake up, rise, and hunt. So we do that. Day after day. Year after year.

And the hunter does not soften. Our wolf does not slow with age. She grows more ruthless, more cutthroat, and more demanding every setting sun. She needs more. *More glory. More work. More bones.* What used to keep her at bay barely scratches her itch now. We hunt as fast as we spin.

Ghost Women are dying to rest, but our fear of discovery keeps us running. Fraud's shadow looms ever darker. The reward of endless hunting is intoxicating, and in order to maintain the lie we have created, we cannot stop.

We have externalized every single ounce of our worth.

As the hunter grows more ruthless, we learn to shapeshift our identity to keep the baying mob dumb to our flaws, and the wolf well fed.

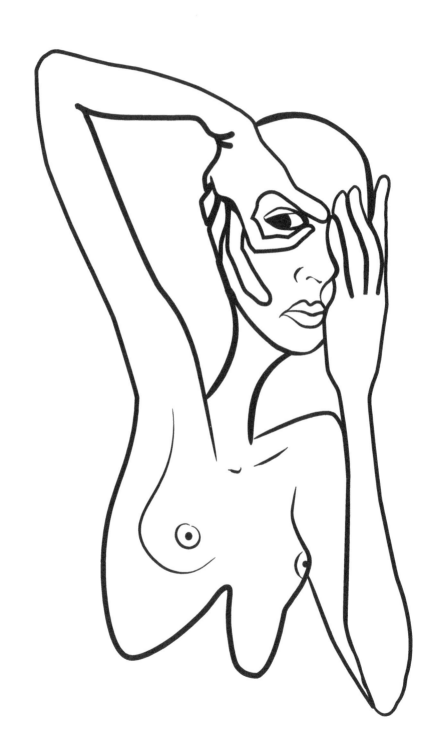

CHAPTER 6

Mask

THE WAYS WE HIDE SO NO ONE HURTS US

———

There is no way to hold a hedgehog. I wore "fuck off" all over my body: every spine a reminder to not get close. What I lacked in size, I make up for in attitude. There's a boldness to my being. Keep a ten-yard radius around me, just in case I charge.

I wonder if I was born with spikes. Or if they grew, sharp and urgent, as I realised no one was coming to hold my hand. That all the ways I sparkled and shone made it impossible for anyone to believe that I cried, too.

They rest under my skin. My default. My armour. A silent but efficient arsenal of sharp needles. Creators of distance.

I feel them corkscrewing through me every time I am reminded that I am a daughter to a mother and a father who did not know how to love me the way I needed.

Wonderful and kind people. With a quiet bomb dropped in their laps.

Thirty-one years old, and years of healing. And boom. Someone's words nick me just enough to bleed and I am eight again. The spines shoot through my skin. I curl up in a ball. Tight, alone, and small.

A reminder of the days I hugged myself between the radiator and the back of the sofa because you did not know how to hold me. You didn't think I needed holding.

The Hedgehog daughters.

Were we born this way? Were we made this way? Perhaps a bit of both. Perhaps there is small comfort in knowing we are everywhere.

I feel them still. All over my heart, and under my skin. The nubs of spines that guard a soft underbelly. An underbelly I am slowly learning is safe to show.

THE WAYS WE HIDE

On the surface, Ghost Women appear strong. Fast-talking, shit-talking women who don't need anything from the world but a firm mattress and cold coffee. Those watching and admiring us experience this bold confidence as our essence. They could not be more wrong. When someone encounters a Ghost Women's strength they are interacting with our defense mechanisms. When they feel the full force of our capacity for work, shake our firm hands, and wonder how we do it on four hours of sleep, they are not meeting us. They are meeting all the ways we protect ourselves. They are meeting our masks. The characters we have crafted to smother our pain.

When there is nothing to fear, there is no need to protect. For a Ghost Woman, life without fear is a fairytale. Fear is our guardian. The fuel to keep up the perfect performance for those who watch. We are terrified of the unravelling. Our castle dissolving into sand. What Ghost Women fear the most is people seeing our bald, shorn, unmasked face. In all our pathetic and imperfect glory.

BUTTER

In my early twenties, I lived in Austin. I was not built for the South. The hot sun dulled me.

I was the fattest I had ever been. Sweat sat in new folds. My body showing me where I was wrong.

I found someone to live with through a friend of a friend. I struck gold. A loud and fun woman who, to this day, is my best friend. We lived in a little bungalow with her two dogs and two cats. There was a lot of animal fur.

A weird little man lived in a small house in our garden. He sometimes drove me to work.

It was Sunday and I was binging. Yet another final feast. I walked the seven short minutes to the grubby local store. I bought a tray of sixteen cinnamon rolls, a big bag of crisps, and some pints of ice cream. That should be enough to pass out.

I woke up later in the afternoon. My body wet on my sheetless blow-up mattress. Drool sticking my face to the pillow.

I pulled on a baggy sweatshirt and walked to the store again.

I was at the tipping point. I was sick of eating but wanted to keep going, knowing I would have to starve tomorrow. I walked the aisles waiting for something banned to catch my eye. Nothing looked good.

I thought of how to get the most calories in me.

Punishment.

I bought a box of butter and a family-sized packet of salty crackers. I went home and dipped dry crackers into melting butter until I could not eat one more. I passed out and slept through the night.

My morning shit was rancid. A painful fatty landslide.

I got in his car for the Monday commute.

"Crackers and butter?" he said, his eyes on the road. "Yum."

I froze.

"I saw you at the store yesterday."

I could feel my cheeks. Already puffy from sugar. Like red clown balls.

Butter and cracker bile in my throat.

Did he know?

Could he see?

I felt the blush rising. Prickling heat crawling up my throat.

"I bake," I said quickly.

"Cool."

I could feel the sweat running down my forehead.

I started ordering food online after that.

You never know who is watching.

What they see.

The thought of this man knowing how fucked I was felt like death. Ghost Women fear nothing more than others seeing through us.

And really seeing us.

We fear them seeing all the pockets where fat sits on our undisciplined bodies. Our soft and sad folds. Our hairy and smelly ordinariness. The risk is high. The thought is unbearable.

Like slicing a baby's neck.

Ghost Women have everything to lose. So we find ways to act strong. To feel impenetrable. We develop a complex array of masks to protect our true self. Masks help us hide within our tortured charade. A mask is the opposite of an invitation. It is a directive. *Do not come near me.* Masks are the way we put our fear to work by externalizing our inner pain. We wear our cunty and cold masks like second skin. A conscious distancing from, and defense against, truth.

Putting on a mask and playing a role is the perfect way for Ghost Women to manufacture a barrier between how we feel inside, and how others experience us. Masks let us teach people how they are allowed to interact with us.

THE CAST

Clowns are the saddest people. A Ghost Woman's fate is worse because there is a deftness to the way we paint our masks. There is an art to the desperation of our sorcery, and our performance is anything but one note. We choose different masks depending on the setting to control how others act. Outcomes range from fear, to submission, to awe. We enroll our audience to the circus. *Buy our tickets. Watch our show!* And we make sure we give them a show worth watching.

My masks made me feel powerful when I felt most broken.

They gave me confidence when I was on the brink of tears and made me feel important, safe, and protected.

I wore many masks over the years. There was a consistent theme: darkness.

BLACK SHEEP

Growing up, I loved the role of the Black Sheep. I enjoyed the benefits of looking and acting like the odd one out. I felt special, different, elevated. A true middle child. I shaved my head before a dance performance when I was very small. A thick band of elastic pinning the oversized bow close to my skull. I looked ridiculous. But I did not look like anyone else.

As I grew older, this mask morphed into the perfect way to garner sympathy and awe. When I moved to America, I stepped off the plane and into a country where my accent made me endlessly fascinating. A curio. A guaranteed topic of conversation. I would chuckle at the dumb Yanks as they tried to woo me with stories of their Scottish ancestors. Fawning over how brave I was to leave my family across the ocean.

"Your parents never visit you?" They dug into me. The clingy eyes of needy parents who drove ten hours to see their daughter sit on the sidelines every week. I would act coy and cast my eyes down. Drink their sympathy syrup. *Look how brave she is. How alone she is.* This lone wolf. I felt like an exotic bird on endless display. A flamingo in a sea of city pigeons. The significance of victimhood made the Black Sheep one of my favourite masks to wear.

UNAPPROACHABLE

At work, I was unapproachable. I loved staring through people. They weren't worth seeing until they proved otherwise. The power of this mask was limitless. It gave me a feeling of reverence, and superiority. One of my first jobs was at Google. While all my peers worked and played hard together, I worked hard and alone. I did not speak to people for months. But I made sure they felt my presence.

One weekend, I was hit by a car while riding my bike. The force flung me over the handlebars. My body smacked the road as cars drove around me.

I went to work the next day. My standing desk was in the corner, and I didn't speak to most people. So most didn't notice my face covered in road burn until lunch time.

Gasps. Audible gasps.

It felt amazing to brush off the questions and the fawning and go back to work. The mask's cold nature kept people at a distance, and in awe.

I had a stage. They were my audience. I did not sign autographs for just anyone. *Know your fucking place.*

The mask kept people intimidated and less likely to try to know me. This was good. The closer people were to me, the more vulnerable my armour. Sometimes I would thaw, but it was rare. And only after I assessed their danger. Even still, they got a highly curated experience of me.

BITCH

She was on the team at Syracuse. She did not look like a hockey player. Tall. A little gangly and awkward. Her pale skin burned so easily.

It was the questions that made me hate her. Endless questions. She asked everyone. *What do you think I should do? Can you help me?*

I'd see her eyes darting around. Fearful. Flickering. Always looking for someone to tell her the answer.

So much nervous lip licking.

And the part I could not understand?

Everyone loved her for it.

And the worst part?

She was better at hockey than me.

It did not make sense in my head.

Time to slice and dice.

I talked about her. Loudly. On the bus.

Funny.

Brutal.

I loved being that person. The bitch who said the cruel things most people barely dared to think about.

Until I noticed an untied shoe sticking out into the middle aisle of the bus. She was sitting right in front of me.

I got really quiet.

It took her a few days. She finally asked to talk to me.

She sat across from me. Her watery eyes and blubbery mouth. Gunk stuck in the corners from anxious licking. Yesterday's dinner crusted on her top. Sleep in her eyes.

I could not look into those eyes.

I could not say a word.

I knew I was wrong.

I could not say sorry.

I remember thinking my mum would be so ashamed of me.

But as shame washed over me I found no other option. No other way to feel strong.

So I kept talking about her, just not on the bus.

Masks don't teach you anything about being human.

METHOD ACTING

The ways masks protect us are entwined with why Ghost Women shrink. Shrinking to be visible is an expression of internal pain. Our masks are the camouflage we wear in public to conceal what sits below the surface. Masks are our reaction to the ways we were not loved, the ways we were not held, and the ways we were not acknowledged. Putrid and unprocessed poison.

Eating barely enough requires effort. By comparison, wearing a mask is effortless. Masks develop over the years and are intimately connected to our story webs. We turn the stories into personalities and, in time, slip into our roles with ease.

Masks give us a safe way to act in the world. An embodied defense mechanism that helps Ghost Women to hide in plain sight. Our audience falls for the illusion that the role they watch us play is who we really are.

There is a reason why actors do forty-seven seasons of the same show. They become their character. A Ghost Woman's experience is no different. But we are not getting paid to play our role.

We are paying with our lives.

Playing the Ghost Women is a sick form of method acting. The irony of wearing masks is that our fear of our truth being discovered is enough for us to feel comfortable lying most of the time.

We have no faith we could leave the role and be someone different. Every day, we take another quiet but vicious step in the direction of self-betrayal. We find it more and more difficult to separate the role we play from the mask we wear. The spinning stories wrap around our necks and hang us as the masks melt into our skin.

THE CRITIC

Ghost Women's belief that everyone is watching and waiting for us to fail is a displacement of our inner critic. We project our fears of being caught onto the captive audience who drool if we stumble over our lines. Every day that we stand on stage, we bow to an audience of one.

The cruel judge that sits at the heart of all our suffering is us.

There are enough tragic stories of child actors to know fame, talent, and money is not protective. Invisible Children grow up into Ghost Women with no foot grounded in reality. The gift is the poison. We succumb to playing a drugged, dazed pawn in our own game.

Riddled through our numbness, the hunting, the safe distances we keep, and the chilly brush off weaves a soulful yearning. A deep longing to be able to go out without the mask.

Early on in my relationship with my partner, I caught glimpses of what my life could be like if I dropped my act. I was in graduate school. But I had not thought about my career since I met him. He flooded me with hints of fun I had not felt for so long. Maybe ever.

One morning I went to the gym early. I wrecked myself like

I always did. I came back, showered, and walked into his bedroom. He was starting to stir awake.

"What are you doing today?" he asked.

"Working."

My default response.

"Do you want to go on an adventure?"

I did not understand. It was a Wednesday. No one has fun on Wednesday.

"Let's go."

He drove me to a park. Pink blossoms and grassy hills. We sat for hours. He took photos of me and told me I was beautiful. We ate lobster rolls. I could taste the butter.

Such an expensive thing to eat.

It felt like oxygen and like the ocean and like drugs. The unbearable lightness of not counting.

Like grey clouds dropping to cover the sun.

I knew I would have to pay.

Later that day, I biked home.

I did not eat dinner.

CURTAIN CALL

Ghost Women entertain the idea of being normal for a moment before going back to reciting rehearsed lines. The risk of living carefree is too great. We fear what will happen if we stop wearing the masks we know work. We are strangers to our own reflection.

We have no idea who we are.

But take my word on it. You will never heal your invisible pain without taking the masks off. The truth we fear most is the truth that will set us free.

The choice to start peeling off the fake layers of identity requires uncommon bravery. The surrendering of the roles you have acted your whole life will feel like a death. There are days when I miss the darkness of my masks. Working people into the ground. The slant of my unfriendly scowl. Shrinking. I miss being drunk on power. My tiny muscles pressing against fatless skin. I miss running my fingers down my riblets. The left side. The right side. I miss my hungry face. My icy blood. I miss being hell bent on a diet. Purpose coursing through me like murder.

When our reckoning comes we are faced with a choice. Hide, or heal. But hiding in plain sight is hard to let go. We are Stockholm survivors, never brave enough to use the key that always sat deep in our own pocket. We must be ready to mourn the loss of our role. To miss the ways our darkness made us strong. To find a way to be whole that does not require undermining someone else. To let go of the story that our pain is greater and deeper and more complicated than anyone could ever understand.

There will be blood. A lot of it. But honest blood is necessary blood. For every weed we yank, we leave fresh soil.

You have no idea what takes root in the space left behind when suffering vacates.

In choosing to peel off our masks, Ghost Women create space for more of who we are to shine through. And while vulnerability is horrifying, so is the choice to stay invisible.

Ask yourself. Are you okay making your own life miserable? Suffocating yourself? Fighting a war of your own creation? Are you okay never knowing who you really are? Never sharing your true gifts? Are you okay living your life at a safe distance? Being a constant stranger? Are you okay keeping people close enough to watch but not close enough to see through your cracks?

Or can you trade the mask in? For a life that is no longer curated by fear. One fueled by the smoldering embers of freedom.

Masks serve a purpose. They wrap a convenient shell around who we are and what we feel. They help keep up the appearance of strength.

The cost is high. We pay with our whole life.

Ghost Women have spent our whole lives held safe in rigid control. Numb and dumb.

You have every right to be afraid. In laying down the mask you are opening up Pandora's box. The emotional body.

CHAPTER 7

Beast

WE FEAR OUR BODY'S BETRAYAL

I am drugged to the eyeballs so I don't eat children
But I am not in a zoo
And I gave myself the drugs
I do not know how to be wild
I was built for rolling space
To tear flesh and howl with my sisters
But I do not know how to hunt
I do not know how to sleep
I do not know how to drink the water I crave
And I am scared of my own roar
I say I want the wild lands
I have lost everything that made me wild
sit slumped and full of pre-cut meat
And fear my own teeth
I rule over everything
But my kingdom is a prison

I think I want to be wild
But I cower at my own shadow
I am scared of everything that lives
Trapped inside this cage

CAGE HER

Ghost Women operate under the pretense of confidence and brutal efficiency. On face value, we fear no one, and we do not have anything to be scared of. Our bluster is built on a fortress of fear that centres around a lack of safety feeling, or expressing our emotions.

We see self-mastery as an emotionless state, because we do not believe love and admiration exists unless we are perfect. We have no idea how to open up. To say what is true, or disappoint other people. To admit weakness. To lose. To be bad. To be wrong. We also have no idea how to surface our own humanity, wrap arms around our pain, and weep.

We build a cage to trap the beast.

Pain bubbles inside us. The only way to cope is to externalize our internal turmoil in appropriate ways by pouring our fear, self-hatred, and coarse unworthiness into shrinking and working for worth. This smart redirection of energy gives us, and the world, fake evidence that we are the pinnacle of our species. A woman who has transcended emotions. A robot. A locked cage. In control. *Doing it right.*

Who cares if we rip our own heart out in the process?

Willpower is a muscle. It tires and tears when overworked. And our pain boils. Ghost Women are dancing around a sleepy volcano of unprocessed and unacknowledged emotional energy. We fear taking our masks off. We are scared to death of our emotional body and what might happen if the top blows.

FOUR YEARS

Sometimes, we will stoop very low to quiet the beast.

I dumped her over the phone while she was on a work trip. I still remember her saying, "What do you mean?" Her quiet voice strangled and small.

You would think someone you have spent four years of your life with deserves better.

She did deserve better.

But the beast was stirring in me.

I met her in college. She was tiny and blonde. Perfectly in proportion. Breasts that looked good in a white shirt with no bra. She liked her body. And she knew how to eat. Bread. Cheese. Butter on everything.

I sometimes think I dated her so I could see what I did not have.

I had not dated a woman before. But she worshipped me. Everything about me. It was so easy. She saw me tiny, and she saw me puffy and fat with binges, and for some reason she didn't care.

And the best part? We never fought. No raised voices. No conflict. I could not do wrong to her. We glided through years in a perfectly quiet space. I thought that was it. *I mastered love.*

No truth. Just niceness. And agreement. Endless agreement. Even when I didn't agree.

Someone who would never leave.

Safe.

And numb. The time felt numb.

Then one day, four years deep, I woke up with flames. Anger so raw and bloody. And the walls of my skull squeezing the juice in my brain.

Get the fuck out.

Get the FUCK out.

I didn't even know what the voice was. Where it came from. It sounded caged and cruel and rageful. Deep inside. Like bile bursting and frothing in a hot cauldron.

I needed it to stop. I needed it to stop right now.

I picked up the phone and called her.

Four years. A three-minute phone call. And I ruined her life for a while.

I felt bad for her. I also felt relieved. The beast lay down again.

QUIET PLACE

Ghost Women see emotionality as a wild animal we must control at any, and all, costs. We have no time in our day for anything that feels wild or unruly. In our eyes, the dread, the sadness, and the incompleteness we feel is evidence of weakness. But at least we are the only ones seeing it.

My parents are good people but they did not teach me how to voice feelings in a healthy way. My whole life was even keel. No raised voices or visible disagreements. No talking about emotions. Zip it shut. Sweep it under the rug. God is good.

I learned conflict is dangerous. Emotions are unsafe. Do everything to be perfect so you can feel nothing.

I spent so many years keeping everyone I viewed as worthless at a distance. But the few people I let in? I lay down like a fucking doormat. No fights. No conflict. Just, "Yes, that sounds nice." Perfect quietness. If I ever felt conflict stirring, I would leave. Working through an emotion with someone else felt unsafe and impossible.

Never mind working through an emotion with myself. That's when I would train for hours. Or binge. Or drink three litres of water.

I couldn't do it. Voice the pain. I couldn't do it when I got one question wrong in a test. When the boys called me "I-own-a dick" in the playground and whispered "hermaphrodite" in my ear. I couldn't do it when the pressure to win prizes paralysed me. I couldn't do it when my eating was out of control. I couldn't do it when my parents never visited me in America. When no one came to my graduation.

It didn't matter. I wasn't bothered. *It's fine.* Opening my eyes so wide hoping the air would dry the brewing tears. Waking up in the night grinding my teeth. Anything to make sure they didn't see me breaking. *Broken.*

But I watched them my whole life. Pathetic women. Trembling, crying, and needing someone to hold them. Every time my sister was excused. Average celebrated. This raw and gaping display of fragility met with deep love. I would freeze in place. Bearing down. Feasting for a second on the weakness. Shaming them as my body flooded with a raw yearning for how gently they were held. Gazing at them through the longing eyes of a child who never learned if love existed in spite of weakness.

SMOTHER

Ghost Women are fighting for our lives. For our survival. Our sense of safety centres on our ability to control our emotions. The orchestration of the dance is complex, cold, and efficient. As long as we shrink, we make ourselves visible in the way we desire. As long as we are perfect, we are impenetrable. As long as we feel nothing, and show nothing, we are safe.

We believe vulnerability is the same as weakness, and emotions are the gateway drug. Over the years, we have built a stoic prison to hold the tides of emotions that stand to ruin our carefully curated presentation of strength. We have caged the beast.

I remember waking up for weeks in a row with dark and solid self-hatred pushing down on me like I was trying to smother myself with a pillow. My lungs filled with hate-laced acid and I lay there struck by my ability to make myself feel so terrible. It was terrifying and, in the same breath, a waste of my time.

I had no time to entertain the drama. I swallowed the hatred over and over again. If I didn't, I would be late to the gym.

Emotions are like experiences. They need to be aired, and felt. They want to resolve. Ghost Women never let our feelings see the light of the day. Instead, pain loops in chaotic and scary cyclones deep inside. We grow more and more terrified of the beast that stalks our cage. We are furious at how hungry she is, and how deeply she feels. But there is no planet in a universe where we feel safe to unlock the cage and set her free.

Ghost Women are not stupid. We feel the centre of the storm nearing. All we can do is buckle down harder to control our ugly and craven urges. We clamp hands over intuition's mouth and shame her as the needy voice of our untrustworthy body. In our sickness and sadness, the only visceral feedback we love and depend on is the rumbling of our empty stomach.

Our hunger and our binges serve similar but different purposes: the starving or smothering of our emotional body. As loud as the beast roars, the rattle of a hungry body stands as proof. That our cage is strong enough to imprison our weakness.

TRANQUILIZE

I was cutting weight for a weightlifting competition. I always chose one weight class down so I had a reason to starve harder.

The weight cut was working. My muscles and bones were rising to the surface like a sunken wreck.

I woke up early to plan my day down to the calorie. My coach would be waiting for me in a badly lit stony alcove at the back of a CrossFit gym. Every morning at six-thirty.

He was Russian. He didn't say much. But he said a lot.

"Closer." A quick nod.

Bumper plates and cold metal bars.

Thick calluses.

Bruises ringing my clavicle like a noose.

I looked down at my shins. Identical scars running down the front. Crusty scabs. Ready to rip. I felt its rusty path grating up my legs as I pulled the bar off the floor. Tearing.

I could not tell if the blood on the bar was mine or borrowed.

"Not bad."

I shoved my hand in the chalk bucket and rapped the white powder onto the open wounds.

"Again."

The pain was sick. I loved it.

The weeks would drag on as competition day drew near.

Crying. I would cry every day, but only when I was lifting. That was allowed.

Hunger is hard. It makes time very long. I would haul myself to the gym every morning and feel nothing but a deathly quietness sitting in my bones. Inside, a witch cackling at how good I was doing.

I had reached the edge of the world. Beyond hunger.

Binges were a different road to an eerily similar destination. As soon as my weightlifting competition was over I got home, put on my tightest and smallest clothes and walked to the local burger bar. Bacon. Double cheddar. Mayo. Ketchup. Extra chips. Salt vinegar. I almost ran back to my flat.

There is nothing like thick salty grease after months with an empty fridge.

Slamming the door as I ripped open the paper bag and shoved my first meal in months in my face. My tummy straining within minutes after so many weeks of dollhouse portions.

A cow eating a cow. I swallowed the burger in massive chunks, and chugged a milkshake until milk sunk through my eyeballs and washed my brain in a meaty stupor. My veins electric with sugar.

I had reached the edge of a different world. Tranquilized. Numb in a different way.

All the weight I lost over two months came back in less than a week. My stomach strained with half-chewed food and trapped gas. My mornings smeared with painful, creepy liquid shits.

That was the thing about starving. It worked until it didn't.

Then I would sit slumped in the corner of my cage and let the freakshow roll.

We are scared of the hell in our bodies. We are scared of the bloody pulsing ox heart punching our ribcage. We fear the smell, and the hair, and the teeth, and the guts. We fear wild rapids flooding our throats. We fear the curdling anger that broils our guts. Choking on the stick-like bodies of moths. An anger that is raw and dusty and old.

We fear our friends, family, and foes standing agog, jaws hanging, popcorn in hand, unable to peel their eyes away from our tragic reveal. The hysteria. The heat of embarrassment and the depth of failure. Our only hope is to pray to gods that don't exist that beasts can't chew through steel.

SCRAPBOOK

Energy is never destroyed, only redirected. Emotions are no different. Stuffing, swallowing, or suppressing a short-term solution for masking long-term terror. A Band-Aid on a bullet wound. A moment of nothingness. Temporary relief before the blood starts seeping through.

By ignoring our emotional pain, Ghost Women think we are dealing with "it."

We are not dealing with it.

Our bodies become a living and breathing museum of crimes against the self. A revelry of abandonment. A scrapbook of betrayals.

The Ghost Woman's ignored feelings, traumas, and desires don't go anywhere. Emotional pain sits in our bodies and over time compacts and morphs together, in the same way a volcano erupts and settles into itself. Wounds upon wounds upon wounds. Never cleaned. Never aired. Never healed.

The suppression of emotion is a sickness. Feelings rot and fester inside us. The beast we've drugged for years grinds awake and starts hurling herself against the bars of our cage.

Our emotional pain has to surface in some way. Our beast finds new throats to roar her wrath. Stifled emotions manifest physically. Sore throats, blood-thirsty periods, digestion problems, constricted breathing, never-ending colds, allergies, breakouts. The emotional pain we've swallowed starts leaking poison into our cells. Our bodies writhe and bubble.

TEETH

Like rotten eggs in warm sun. I could taste it every time I breathed. The stink built over months. I'd scrub my mouth raw in the mornings. Chew a new piece of gum every ten minutes. But it clung. To the roof. Lodged in the corners and in the folds.

One day, I bent down into a forward fold at the gym. I heard a tiny pop, and tasted sour gunk. Like an old juicy spot on an old man's hairy back. I spat on my hand. Yellow chunky pus.

I brought my finger to my nose. It smelled like a dump. Putrid rotting fat on a cold stove top.

I did it to myself.

The binges.

I rarely brushed my teeth at night. I'd grab food and head to the bedroom and shove it in my mouth quickly before my partner came in. Or I would fall asleep watching television, sleepy on sugar. I'd wake up in the middle of the night. My tongue thick with a layer of stink, my bra biting into my back as I dragged myself into bed before my alarm went off at five o'clock in the morning.

My gums throbbing. Ulcers covered my tongue with prickling polka dots. White and stabbing. My tongue swollen and red. I could not bring myself to go to the dentist.

The shame choked me. I held onto it. The pain I deserved.

There is only so much emotional pain we can endure before our body cannot take it anymore. No matter how tightly we cling, the cage we live in is no competition to the oceans of pain we've bathed our souls in for years.

Our body feels like she's dying. But our body is on our side. She finds a way to break the cage so we finally pay her the attention she needs. That we need.

INTO THE WILD

It is easy to pathologize the body as the root of our suffering. We have fabricated years of evidence to prove we cannot trust her. As our emotional pain intensifies, our beast is the obvious source to blame. We lie again.

Our body is not to blame. The opposite. We are the ones who

have weaponized our mind through fear. We are the ones guilty of committing war crimes against ourselves.

Ghost Women fear the beast who lies drugged in our cage. We cower at the ways she makes us feel. We do not trust that in her wildness we can find answers. That by setting her free we do the same for our whole self.

We are the beast. We are the cage.

But we were not created for small spaces. We were not born to fear ourselves. Coincidence is a lie. Our souls chose these bodies for a reason. A reason that cannot be found in the nutritional information on the back of a cereal packet. We shrink and hope for power and love and freedom in our smallness. It is nowhere to be found because in our hearts we do not crave small.

We crave ourselves.

Our only job is to find the heart to heal our body's broken bonds. We must set the beast free to learn who we really are.

Like the breeze of another world. A key turning in an old and rusty lock. A remembering. Things shift and come into focus in a way we once knew but long forgot. Your only job is to edge the door of the cage open. And keep it open. To feel the emotions one by one. To heal the body.

This is not how Ghost Women have lived. We have broken nature's rules. We have learned to know better than to listen to impulses. Dangerous. Messy. No guarantee of outcome. There is an arrogance to our minds. A brokenness. Born in repetition and by listening to those who know nothing about what is best for us.

We see the way others go about their lives. We let their brokenness dance with our brokenness. And we grow to believe that we are here to control our variables, manage our weakness, and drug the beast.

We cage early. We cage often. It starts in meddling thoughts, and rivers through our lives like a gutsy plague. The body breaks, or frightens and freezes. The key turns and our beast lies down. Our soul gets quiet.

Counter to all that we have believed to be true, our job is not to be a robot, ruthless in our pursuit of perfect.

Our job is to uncage the beast. To feel. And to really feel. To allow the world to witness our unique expression. To play out our soul's curriculum.

THE CALL

There is only one of you. Ever.

Every single one of us deserves to be remembered.

Let it be for the correct reason. For the true expression of your soul.

You think you fear your beast. You think you need the cage. But what you really need is to have the heart to break free from your invisible prison and learn who you are when you do not shrink. Who you are without the convenient bonds of shame. Who you are without the fear and the fraudulence that keeps you quiet and sad in the corner.

The wild is waiting. You were born for open spaces. The brilliance others see is only magnified by the grace you give yourself to be human.

Healing comes from becoming wild again, like the raucous and rowdy child who at some point along the road got quiet, serious, and sad.

You think you are beyond saving. You are not beyond saving.

The answers are already here.

Do not fear the beast. Fear the life of a beast that stays in her cage.

Be your own prison ward. Or set yourself free.

Leave this cage one step at a time. You can learn to feel again one moment at a time. You can liberate what you have suppressed, denied, and shamed one emotion at a time.

And know this. If you are anything like me, you will crawl back and cower in this cage one hundred times before you leave it. You will drug the beast a million more times. That's okay.

Becoming a Ghost Woman took practice. Becoming the liberator of your soul takes practice, too. Choose to believe that everything you need to feel real is already here. In your hands. Your only job is to set yourself free.

Are you willing?

make yourself real

CHAPTER 8

God

YOU HOLD ALL THE CARDS

———

You are the tiny bird
Tweeting
You are the open palm
Twitching
Learn
Not to crush
Your own bones

TINY BIRD

Controlling our reality has no place in making the Ghost Woman real. But trust is the opposite of what we have practiced. We only know a world where rigidity, control, and efficiency are the safe expression and conservation of identity. At the expense of being a real person, we strive to be a perfect one. We disappear completely. When a Ghost Woman chooses to make herself real, all she knows is to shrink. That will not work anymore.

We have caged our bodies and soul in pursuit of perfect. We have little to show but pain. Healing does not happen inside cages. Force and control do not build trust. But faith and hope do not heal our invisible pain either. Healing is not a surrendering of self to the ether. It is not "hands in the air and take me." Healing our invisible suffering is a conscious and continual commitment to being seen. It requires bravery and practice and patience. Uncommon amounts.

Ghost Women have little to no evidence that we deserve to live without suffering. We must become as ruthlessly committed to practicing vulnerability as we have, until now, relied on strength. The energy to support this shift comes from aligning ourselves with what we desire most, to rendering ourselves real. It is not enough for us to gain awareness of our pain and move on. That is not healing, that is a hat tip. Our body is not healed by common courtesy. We are healed through the experience of feeling. Giving ourselves time and space to realise what we have done, and why. That requires vulnerability. Oceans of it.

We have never lived in open space. All we know are hunger, stories, masks, and cages. In choosing a new way, we must create space between who we are now, and what we desire to be. A safe, liminal space to practice being, and feeling, real.

The space that holds you heals you.

You must make the space first. And get comfortable resting in it. The caterpillar needs the cocoon. She cannot fly without it. The embryo needs the womb. The baby grows wise and small as if by magic, but she needs the space to curl up. The arm needs the cast. The cast holds no magic. The bones know what to do. Sleep holds you in rest. Your body is the one breathing life through your weariness.

Imagine you are a tiny bird resting in your open palm. The bird sings a beautiful melody. Ruffling a plume of bright blue feathers. But you can't help yourself. You are scared this perfect little bird will fly away, lost forever. Your hand starts closing and you crush the bird. Gently at first, but then bones start to crack, her eyes bulge and burst with blood, and the tiny bird goes limp in your grasping fist. You open your palm too late. Her skull is broken.

You are this bird. You are also this hand. For Ghost Women, crushing the beauty of our own life is a well-worn path. Bound by control. Dreaming of freedom while throttling our chance to live. We must find a way to still the twitching palm.

I work with many creative women. One took magical photos of her home city. A rich mash-up of urban burnished concrete and luscious jungle. Her long cheekbones and dark piercing eyes in frame but minimised. Her body. *Small. Alone.*

The work was beautiful. It was not her soul's work. She found herself fixated on other artists, desperately copying them and their promise of guaranteed beauty. Her own channel was shut tight through years of pain. Her dad's tough voice telling her to hurry up. Her mum, brisk and scared. "The world is not a good place."

She spent her whole young life shrinking to stay safe. Creating other people's art but rarely her own. Scared of everything. Fear lingering around every corner.

It took more than she wanted. But as she softened her fist, her soul shone through like hazy sunbeams.

We cannot live with stiff hearts. Moving from a clenched to open palm gives Ghost Women a fighting chance to allow our soul to illuminate the way it wants to. We must allow the tiny bird to fly. We must trust that she will come home in the end, and accept she may fly a different direction than our minds want her to.

CONTROL AND BLIND FAITH

Living with our hands wrapped around our own throats makes freedom of expression impossible. The natural lightness of our human nature spoils and rots as we suffocate to stillness. Life leaks out of us like a rusty tap. The mirth. The joy. The cheekiness. I grew up knowing I was darkly funny, but I'll never forget the night nobody laughed.

KIMCHI

We sat crammed into a small and dark room. Our teacher

was a small wiry man who made a lot of bad sex jokes. He worked part time at a sauna and did stand-up late at night.

One evening, we were playing a game of assumptions. It was supposed to give us ideas for jokes about ourselves.

We had to go around the circle and say what we assumed about each person based on appearance alone.

I felt quite at home.

Until it got to me. I looked around the room of mostly men daring them to go there.

They went there.

"You're uptight."

"I think you're a bitch."

"You take yourself so seriously."

"You might be an assassin."

"You think you're fucking great."

"You're not funny. At all."

"I don't think you have any friends."

A week or two later, we had to share our first joke. I had not had time to prepare. Every morning and night I was at the gym, and the rest of the day I was at work.

I'm funny. I'm fucking smart. So I winged it.

I stood up and started telling a joke about a dog named Kimchi who was rescued from a Korean meat factory. I stumbled over two or three lines before the sweat began pouring down my face.

I was seven again. The blush of a wrong sum ripping through me.

My hands shaking.

I looked around the room.

Stone-cold stares.

I started another sentence and trailed off. I had nothing to say.

I scanned the room again. All these dumb men and boring women who I had not bothered to tell my name. I stared at them. Begging them to laugh.

This is what it feels like to plead.

Even the teacher could not summon kindness.

I could feel the tears boiling.

I sat down quickly.

My crack was soupy with sweat.

You fucking stupid cunt.

I could still feel it the next morning. The shame afterglow.

I biked to the gym at dawn to burn it off.

I never went back.

I had always thought I was hilarious and brilliant off the cuff. That night, I caught a glimpse of just how tightly closed my fist was. How unlikeable I was.

BLIND FAITH

Ghost Women are gripped so tightly by fear that our lives ice over into endless robotic days. Calculated and executed with no colour in sight. Our worth confined to the size of our waist and the calories in gum. How many hours we have worked, and the number nestled between our toes on the scale. I look back and want to weep at how much space shrinking took up in my life. My whole life, all my energy, and all my strength. Art, humour, writing, and fun. Withered. Rotten. Dead.

Ghost Women believe a tightly managed presentation of who we are, and a relentless commitment to "more" guarantees our survival. Control is the paradigm we've bought into and fed on. But control is a fragile construct built on a foundation of fear. Control has a tightness that allows no space for everyday magic.

I could not go for nights away without researching nearby gyms. If my partner sprung a date on me I would immediately go to the bathroom, find the restaurant website, and decide which meal would not completely ruin my week.

Fist. Closing.

Ghost Women fear that in surrendering our extremes we will collapse into lazy heathens. Bovine and sick and average. What we judge in others, we fear for ourselves. So we squeeze ourselves to death until we lie dry and crusty in the desert. An orange peel twisted and purged of juice by a cruel sun.

Our energy gets stuck within walls we've built. Slowly shrinking the space we have to live in. The theme of our thoughts is fear. Unworthiness dripping and filling every cell of our being with limitation. We end up creating a hell far worse than the most violent prison: a boring, small one. A succession of swampy grey days to wade through until we die.

The opposite of control is blind faith. But faith is a loaded term for anyone who has banked significant evidence of suffering. What the fuck should we have faith in? Ghost Women swing to the other side and fully embrace the delicious blackness of nihilism. Faith also carries a religious bent. A promise that rarely makes sense for Ghost Women who have always seen the world a little too clearly.

I was raised in a religious home. My parents induced my birth so my dad could concentrate on his ministry exams. I hated church. I cringed listening to the dusty fairy tales every Sunday. I shuddered hearing my mum's tone-deaf singing and cringed as I watched my sister raise her hands and sway to gospel choruses. Instead, I sat at home poring over dinosaur skeletons in old printed encyclopedias. I loved asking my mum what Jesus had to say about stegosauruses.

Questioning is a core tenant of a quick mind. Ghost Women

have it in spades. For years, my jaw twitched every time I heard an athlete thank Jesus after a game. "Where's God now?" I asked, huffy, when the librarian at our school died and I watched her five kids sitting weeping in the church pews.

Blind faith is no different than iron-clad control. The reincarnation of the victim in a gentler way. I resented seeing smart people handing their lives over to God's will. I did not see the surrender as beautiful. I saw it as lazy. *Why don't you give a fuck?* I still do not like organized religion: the hypocrisy and the judgement of different types of love makes me boil. But there is a bigness, a boldness, and a beauty to the idea that our actions are supported by energy that is not human.

INVENTORY

In a Ghost Woman's healing journey, control gets you nowhere. Neither does blind faith. So shoot for the middle. Fuck the numbers. Fuck the timeline. Believe, instead, that you have influence.

You must start to loosen your fist by first accepting where you are, what you have done. Then giving yourself permission to try a new way.

Acceptance. Permission. Acceptance. Permission. Acceptance. Permission.

Repeat this until you are you.

Acceptance may look very different for every Ghost Woman: it depends on your particular strain of invisible pain. When

I chose to make myself visible I knew I had to stop all forms of dieting. I was terrified. I did not know what I looked like fed. Every part of me believed I would balloon, and my worth would vanish. Gone in mere moments.

I had to see the writing on the wall. One day, I wrote down every single diet I had started, approximately what year, the type of restriction, and what foods I banned. I noted if I lost weight and if I gained the weight back. I searched for an event that kick-started the diet in the first place.

At a certain point, the ink ran out. The point was made. I had tried over one hundred times to change my life by dieting. Every single time, the diet had not worked.

It is the definition of insanity to do the same thing one hundred times expecting a different answer.

Fear makes brilliant women dumb.

Logic won't heal you. We can't think our way through pain. But, sometimes, it takes seeing sad repetition to illuminate our closed fist.

Was I embarrassed by my failures? Yes. Was I scared to stop dieting? Yes. Was I terrified of gaining weight? Yes. Did I have to? Probably. We cannot change what we have not first accepted. I accepted in that moment that I was no longer a woman who could diet.

I threw out all my weapons: the scales, measuring cups, tracking apps, and skinny clothes. I gave myself complete permission to eat anything at any time. I accepted that my body would change and my only job was to be there for myself.

It sometimes takes months from the moment a woman says she wants to stop shrinking to actually commit. There is a reason why Ghost Women stay invisible. It is fucking terrifying to let go.

But transformation gains ground through trust, and trust is earned on the battlefield. We can't be a philosopher of healing. We need skin in the game. We must be willing to take action in the absence of evidence that we will succeed, and trust that we are supported. By aligning our energy in the direction of healing, Ghost Women become the destroyers of our old lives, and the creators of new ones.

Choosing to rest on acceptance and permission marks a shift from a hunted self to a healing self. Learning how to live with an open palm is foreign. Healing takes hold when we create space to suspend the pain of our reality long enough to imagine a life where we are visible. Where we do not shrink. Where our healing has already happened.

FUTURE SELF PROJECTION

Universal energy is a creative and suspended forcefield. What is true for nature is true for us: energy is never destroyed, only redirected. When we align ourselves with what we desire, and create the space to practice vulnerability, we cannot fail to heal.

Time is passing with or without you. Your life panning out in the direction your energy is placed. The only thing you have influence over is where you direct your energy, and what you believe is available for you.

Make a choice.

The first step towards rendering ourselves real is imagining a reality where our healing has already happened. This is called the Future Self Projection. The Future Self Projection is the North Star for healing. I like to think of Simba lying in the whispering grass. Seeing his father looking down on him from the night sky.

Remember who you are.

Our Future Self Projection is our guide when we feel weak and want to scamper back to the shiny lies and old tactics we have used to hide our pain. Employ the dream. Make her work for you.

In creating a vision of your future self, you will get caught in nature's endless circle of birth and death. What we focus on expands, and we cannot create our new reality using the same tools we used to destroy ourselves.

Here is the truth you don't want to hear. There is sacrifice in healing. Deep fucking loss. Get ready to grieve the dizzy highs of shrinking. The crushing shame of failure. You will lose part of who you are because you cannot heal and get everything you want and keep everything that you were. In learning a new way, you must gently let go of the old.

DARK MATTER

I used to focus a lot of energy on death. I had recurring visions of how dramatically and gloriously I could die. They ranged from car crashes to murders where I fought my assailant valiantly but succumbed in tragic and brutal ways.

Sometimes, I imagined walking quietly into a forest knowing I never intended to walk back out. I would dream of news coverage, people discovering my latent genius woven through my personal belongings. An enormous funeral. Everyone weeping that my gifts were taken too soon from an undeserving world.

I used my mind as a weapon to create visions dark and bereft of hope. While I did not die, all my energy was directed to loop in suffering. Do not get caught using your past as a weapon, or as proof that you will fail. When our thoughts are cast under a darkly destructive spell, our energy loops in barren fields. Recreating pain.

I have worked with many women who want to focus on weight loss in their Future Self Projection. The belief that shrinking will make us visible is entrenched. Our desire to shrink will find ways to trick us into believing that we can lose weight in an enlightened way. These are beautiful lies: a Future Self Projection of the unconscious and destructive kind.

If we care about healing, we have to make a conscious choice to create loops of light. And really commit. Because if we continue to focus our energy on shrinking, spending our time recreating suffering, and worshipping the lies that keep us invisible, we will never heal.

NORTH STAR

Our mind has a shadow. She also has access to the brightest of light. Our mind is a magpie. A collector. A tinkerer. Left to her own devices, she will latch and loop our energy in ways that ruin us. But when we are able to shift our mind from a weapon to a wand, she becomes our biggest ally, supporter, and advocate. We can learn to harness the brilliance of our imagination to cast a vision that sets us free.

Create your North Star. Have the bravery, clarity, and conviction to claim what you want for your life and embody the vision on a deep, energetic level. We must find a way to bathe our bodies in possibility. To orient our energy towards what we desire most. Freedom from our own bond.

START NOW

The Future Self Projection takes the form of a letter written by our future self, to our current self. By suspending yourself in the energy of tomorrow, you begin to shift your creative force field in the direction of healing. The letter should focus on how you feel a year in the future.

Light does not capture us the same way pain does. Your vision must take your breath away.

A manifesto of freedom.

Paint it. Make a playlist. Turn the volume up until it hurts. Do whatever it takes for your healing to punch you in the guts in a good way.

In creating a vision of a future you, you create a wise and

aligned resource to support your path to visibility. Your Future Self acts as a wise visionary who you can turn to for inspiration when you are lost or do not feel brave.

Your letter will look nothing like mine. This is what I wrote when I started my work.

Iona,

We did it.

For the last fifteen years, a day did not go by where you did not use food to numb your emotions. There has not been a day where you haven't ruined a beautiful moment with a binge. There has not been a day you haven't trained with the sole purpose of trying to get smaller. There has not been a day that wasn't made, or broken, by the way you felt about your body.

Not anymore.

I'm so proud that you put your ego aside and got the help you needed to reconnect your mind and body.

I'm so proud that you made yourself extremely uncomfortable and confronted the shit you needed to confront.

I'm so proud you learned the difference between emotional and physical hunger.

I am so proud that you rule your own life. Not food.

I'm so proud you've learned strong coping strategies for when shit does happen.

I'm so proud you learned how to reward yourself in meaningful ways.

I'm so proud you stopped undermining yourself and your achievements.

I'm so proud you stopped using exercise to compensate for your food choices.

I am so proud you live in a body that you love and that feels like you.

And now, more than ever, you feel free to roam because you are your own home.

You are the sun of your solar system. Bold, quiet, powerful, in flux, but burning so brightly you can't help but make the right moves. Your pull is strong. What you call out for gravitates towards you. You are exactly where you need to be; in the middle of what matters most.

Thank you for believing in me.

I always knew that we could do it.

Iona

WAND

Do not fall into the trap of using your Future Self to shame your current self. It is easy to feel sad about how far away she feels.

Stop. She is already here.

Waiting for you to be brave.

Your mind is a weapon or a wand. Make yours a force for good. Your body does not know time, only sensation. Every day you must commit to embodying the energetic state of a woman who is no longer a Ghost. Act like her. Speak like her. Dress like her. When you allow acceptance and permission to fill up your heart, your body experiences a new way of being. You heal in the present moment.

I remember holding my letter six months after I wrote it. I had carried it in an elastic wallet around my neck every day. Nestled up against bank cards and receipts. She was dog-eared and torn from all kinds of weather. Six hundred bike rides. Folded and unfolded many times. Gripped sometimes with pissed off and scared hands. I read her words, my words, and wept at how my world now reflected what had once felt impossible.

Time is passing with or without you giving a fuck about your heart. Our life wanders down a path that we are creating. Consciously or otherwise. Care enough. Care enough about this life you have. Take time to understand what you desire the most. Name it. Trust the energy of your deepest desires, and the commitment to your healing, to take care of the rest.

ALL YOU DESIRE ALREADY EXISTS

It may seem like the road is long, and the destination far in the distance. There is nowhere to go. The freedom you desire already exists. The wisdom rests in your palm, but layers of stories, practiced struggle, coping mechanisms and deep, protective fear have made you deaf.

The work of making your pain visible and rendering yourself real is to simply be. To stay right here. And to listen.

There is nowhere to go, and nothing to do but to practice staying in the only moment that exists. This moment. Sit and listen. Everything else is a distraction. Food, or lack of food, is convenient. Shrinking is convenient. Work is convenient. Believing we will always feel broken is convenient. Borrowing problems from the future is convenient. Ruminating on the past is convenient.

None of it matters. None of it helps. Start small, and practice living in the moment, not in time.

You may be shocked by how difficult it is to sit with yourself. Keep practicing. Try again.

THE ZOO

One day early on in my journey, I was practicing living in the present. Living in the present is impossible when you are a Ghost Woman. All I ever did was live in time: yearning for a past life when I was thinner, or throwing my gaze forward fantasizing about eating my allotted teaspoon of peanut butter after dinner.

"Let's go to the zoo."

I looked at him, rolling my eyes. Such a typical suggestion.

We got in the car. Driving with the windows down. An insect or two splattered on the windshield.

We arrived. It was hardly a zoo. More like a rundown farm park. The sign scratched and old. An honesty box for payment.

I found myself pulling on my shirt. Stretching the cotton so it didn't touch the curve of my stomach. My body was changing very slightly. A waxing moon. I felt the fat in the way my cheeks hung differently.

Deep breath. I could do this.

I started walking slowly around the enclosures. Some were empty. I kept looking at every single detail. The mangy horns on the goat. The rough unbrushed undercoat of the wild-looking, white dogs. I looked at all the boring birds. I tried so hard to have the wonder of a child. To be nowhere but in the moment.

It felt forced at first.

But then I started enjoying it.

"Look, he's lost half his ear."

Hours passed. But it felt like no time.

Every enclosure. Every feather. Every gnarled hoof.

I found a miracle in it all.

A tiny breadcrumb of evidence.

That I could live here.

In the present.

CONTROL VERSUS INFLUENCE

We are a little closer to God-like when we choose to inhabit our life, rather than running from it. When we breathe into more of who we are, not more of who we think we should be. All the wisdom, and the knowledge, and the love that we require is already here. It lives in you. It lives in me. It was here all along. Watching quietly. Waiting.

You may be lucky enough to find teachers who inspire and delight you. But as you learn to stay with yourself, filter everything through your body and notice if it feels true to you.

The journey is an easy way to talk about transformation. There is nowhere to go. You already live where you are going. Stand in the middle of your life. Worship your own influence. Pray to yourself. Find wonder in the smallest thing. And in standing still, you become magnetic.

I do not like religion. But when I first started my work, there were so many moments I stopped, put my hands on my stomach, breathed deeply into my body, told myself I was okay, and felt salty tears crusting on the corners of my lip. An answer, in kind.

I was in the presence of a god. I was with myself.

In these moments, I thought, fuck. *I am church.*

Standing still sounds easy. It is not easy. You will fall one million times. Will you be the woman who stands up to try one more time? And keep trying one more time? Every time.

Understand that choosing a new way is not choosing the easy way. There will be days and weeks when you forget to cast your eyes upwards to see True North. You will fuck with your food one hundred times before you finally let yourself eat freely.

Kind work is not easy work. Own the power of your influence. Point your heart, your gut, and your brain due north so whatever is supporting you knows you mean business. Watch the world reorient on your axis. In aligning our energy to what we desire, rather than what we fear, we become our own source of inspiration.

People will walk through your doors, but you are your home. It is not about religion, or the stars, or decks of cards. Pray to the heaven in you. And you better be moving your feet.

In mastering the difference between control and influence, Ghost Women flip a switch. We shift from working hard to destroy what imprisons us, to creating what will set us free. We rediscover who we were before the world got its hands on us.

The wisdom of our Future Self can also help heal the oldest parts of us who have been fighting the invisible war since childhood.

By meeting our past, we heal our future.

CHAPTER 9

Child

LEARNING TO PARENT YOURSELF

———

Macaroni cheese
Not peas. No tomatoes
The colour yellow
A crayon clenched in her left hand
Another book, please
This wee ragamuffin
She does not need much
I watch her scampering around outside on the red brick roads
Crouching to grab a ball lodged under a car
A shock of short dark hair
Curling around tiny ears
Culottes, green with white dots
All scuffed knees and rough abandon
Yelling her brother's name
Thirty-seven bruises on her left leg
Forty on her right
But riding a bike was worth it
A cheeky smile wrapping round her cheeks

CHILD · 165

Gran, is the F word fuck?

I feel the grin whip across my face
As I watch the memories

Just as quickly
It fades
When I think about what I did to her

I'll spend the rest of this life
Saying sorry

RUSSIAN DOLL

A baby is loved before her skin makes contact with air. Before she has ever whispered a sound. A baby does not have to prove her right to love. Her mere being takes care of everything. Her bug eyes, tiny nose, and milky soft downy hair. She does nothing but breathe and the world rests at her feet.

In all the ways we shrink to prove our worth, how far we have fallen from this truth.

Ghost Women can learn a lot about innate worth by reconnecting with the child who lives inside. Our Invisible Child did not just run away. There is no moment where we let go of everything that happened when we were small. We do not step over a hard line on the ground. We never outgrow.

BAD GIRL

Some women are brutally betrayed when they are young. Assault. Absence. Adoption. For many, including myself, our experience of pain and shame is more mundane. Wounding still lands and roots in our young bodies. In moments others have long forgotten.

My parents could not afford private school. They paid for it anyway. I don't think my mum bought new underwear for a decade.

I was five. It was my first day at the fancy all-girls school in Glasgow's West End.

The thick green tunic and butterfly neck shirt felt stiff and uncomfortable. I was used to shorts and comfy cardigans.

Mum drove me into the city. It was pouring rain. She walked in with me and we found the classroom and my new teacher. She said goodbye and left.

Everything went quiet.

Dark.

I looked around.

A switch flipped.

I stood up and bolted out the door.

I ran out of the school, down the stairs. My feet slipping on wet cobblestones.

I saw her in front of me. Walking away. Her back against a thundery sky.

I grabbed for her, clinging to her sleeve.

She looked down shocked.

I looked up shocked.

Eyes. Saucers.

Immediately embarrassed.

What was I doing?

She walked me back in. The teacher shaking her head at me. Stern and disapproving.

"She's not normally like this."

I was given a thorough telling off.

I did not like how it felt to be bad. To do something wrong. To be publicly shamed. A few days later, I remember sitting in the classroom surrounded by stencils and coloured pencils and deciding that, from now on, I would be the best at everything. I remember the choice clearly. It was conscious and considered. Necessary. A line drawn in sand.

Perfect. I am perfect.

There is no single moment where we start to disappear. But looking back, I see part of my soul disappear running under rain. Scared, alone, and shamed.

The past rides with us. Or rather, we ride on it. Like a silent steed. Our consciousness is a history book that we do not get to edit. The world sees one of us, but books are made of many pages. Our identity is a sojourn that never sheds a layer. Rather it dives in and around itself. We may feel like a singular woman, but we are a Russian doll. Nested versions bookmarking moments in time. And our smallest dolls are hurting. Badly.

The Invisible Child's pain imprints and loops in our soul's fingerprint. As we grow into Ghost Women, we fight fresh battles upon torn war grounds. Reparenting our inner child is an essential step in a Ghost Woman's journey towards visibility. We must learn to hold her hand and walk her gently towards a world where she gets what she needs without believing she must work for it. A world where she does not have to shrink for love.

THE INNER CHILD

Our inner child lives in the innermost layers of our Russian doll. She is our Peter Pan Paradox: both our oldest and the youngest parts. She is us at our best and worst. When our inner child feels safe and loved, she is a conduit of creativity, intuition, and playfulness. Ghost Women make cruel inner parents. We were not betrayed once. We were betrayed over and over again. First by others, however unintentional, and then by our own hands. We rarely have access to the pure expression of our gifts because our inner child feels the opposite of safe.

Grown up is made up. We are all just wounded children throwing tantrums in adult bodies pretending we should know better because we have been alive a while. We never outgrow our childhood, nor is our past frozen in time. We still see the world through the inner child's lens, and often, it is tainted.

Our wounded inner child leaks and bleeds into how we experience the world, and how we feel about ourselves as we move through life. As you learn to feel your inner child's presence, you will notice the ways she attempts to get her needs met. Sometimes, she whispers or hides from you. Forcing you to care. Sometimes, she throws herself on the floor and roars through you.

My inner child's wounds seeped through all my relationships.

I grew up believing I did not like hugs. That's what everyone told me. I spent most of my early adult life acting tough to mask the needy voice inside me that yearned for physical proof that I was loved. I had to move across the Atlantic Ocean to get a hug.

I never heard my parents argue. I did not witness conflict resolution. Everything was swept under the rug, so crossed words in my relationships shook me to the core. Insecure attachment dug a deep groove in me. I thought arguments signaled the end. If a relationship was not silent, it was broken. The longer my relationships lasted, the more fearful I would grow. If a partner upset me, I zipped my mouth shut and people-pleased so they would not leave.

WISE PARENT

To heal our invisibility, we must make our inner child feel safe. Be the parent we did not have. This work is not about blame. We are not here to shame our caregivers. They did the best they could. It is our responsibility to reparent our inner child, so she does not feel abandoned or unloved anymore. It is also our responsibility to find ways to reawaken the play-fulness and joy that perfection robbed from her. We must give our wounded inner child permission to fail without repercussion, to play with no expectation of victory, and to learn to trust that our love for her is not finite, or conditional.

You have hunted your inner child with knives.

All Ghost Women have. Your inner child has never known whole love. Not from others. Never from us. We get to try anew. You have turned your back and ignored her. Over and over again. There is no reason why she should trust you. Her experience is suspended in time. A portal to when you first started to disappear. It is your job to learn how to comfort your scared inner child and promise that you are never leaving her out in the cold again.

Ghost Women are not practiced patience and gentleness. Our wounded inner child needs both. To that end, teaching flows both ways. We heal through her and she heals through us.

REACH OUT A HAND

The first step of inner child work is connection. Close your eyes and visualize a memory from childhood. Do not hunt. The brightest star will shine for you. You will have plenty of time to meet all the memories that need your attention.

Imagine you are standing ten feet away watching your inner child. Drink in everything about the memory: where you are, what you're wearing, and who you are with? Lean into all five senses and allow the spirit of the memory to wash all over you.

I remember meeting my inner child for the first time. I was young. Maybe five. I was galloping around outside playing goalie with my brother. A cheeky wee tomboy. I was feisty, fearless, and sweet. Watching her, I felt like a foreign kind of love. It came roaring through me like fire licking petroleum. I loved every single thing about this tiny woman. I imagined walking towards her and wrapping her stiff little body in my arms. In time, I felt the ice in her melting. I cried so hard.

I think she cried, too.

I kept a childhood photo on my phone for many months when I first started reparenting. I grew so fond of seeing her happy face.

My inner child was open to knowing me. This is not the case for all women. For many, our childhood is a mystery, especially for those who have blocked it out for good reason. You may not remember anything about your childhood, or you may feel resistance, dislike, and even numbness towards the child inside you. She may reciprocate those feelings. Do not worry. Use this fracture as an opportunity to practice compassion for how deeply you are hurting. For what you have been through together.

Do not force the thaw. We cannot heal the way we were hunted. We cannot expect a child to trust us when we have given her no reason to. If your inner child is unwilling to connect with you, respect her lack of consent and try again tomorrow.

ASK BETTER QUESTIONS

The second step of inner child work is listening. As Invisible Children, we never learned to speak out loud our needs and fears. We learned to shut our own mouths. In your new role as a wise parent, you must give the oldest parts of you the floor. Let her speak.

When you're working with a childhood memory, ask good and kind questions. Over time, once your inner child trusts you, you can ask these questions whenever you feel disconnected from yourself.

What do you need right now?

How can I love you more?

Listen and do not assume the answers. Often, what you will hear are very simple requests. My inner child would whisper, "Hold me," or "I'm tired." I would feel her tiny body sag in my arms, my body flooded with embarrassment at how lonely and hopeless she felt. Have the heart to give her all the love you can. By meeting your inner child's needs, you reduce her reactivity, and increase the security of her attachment. By listening and honouring her, you are sewing yourself back together.

THROUGH HER EYES

The third step of inner child work is channeling. Experiencing our lives through childlike eyes is a beautiful way to reintegrate the unconscious playful parts of us that are starving for air.

Ghost Women can learn so much from young hearts. My niece is one of my favourite teachers. Weather systems move through her body in mere minutes. Hours spent staring at Sammy the Snake. Hands in the mud. Her joy beaming like a lighthouse through a half empty mouth of baby teeth. Then, from nowhere, the world ends and she throws herself on the floor. The definition of a tortured soul.

No one colour could hold her spirit. She is a rainbow of all that feels important and true. A heart that pumps what it feels and is not scared how large it feels. Powerfully in the present moment.

The present is a foreign country for all Ghost Women.

Learn to visit.

My mum loves to tell the story of my "near deaf" experience. Soon after I was born, I failed my infant hearing tests. Beep after beep after beep. Nothing. Doctors were concerned.

I was sent to a specialist. Further investigation found I was not deaf. I was just fascinated by the world around me. The beeps were dull in comparison to everything I was drinking in.

Decades of rules later, no wonder I felt like a stranger.

I had a lot of making up to do.

Endlessly proving our worth steals the glitter of everyday magic. When Ghost Women are fighting ourselves, we do not have room for wild abandon. For imagination. We learn to roll our eyes at wasted time and fear the bravery of lazy spirits, who still want to dance on tables. We worry about being too much of anything unruly so we are, instead, a lot of very little.

I used to love to sew my own clothes, turn my hair into an afro, and paint for hours. So many years of shrinking later, it did not matter that my favourite colour was yellow. I was as scarce with colour as I was with food and love.

In reparenting, we retrain our sense of wonder. Channeling our inner child can reconnect us to our dormant playfulness and creativity. But freedom will feel foreign and uncomfortable when our fear of judgement surfaces.

Carefree is a process. You can start building trust bridges by asking your inner child to choose an activity she would like to do, or what she would like to eat for dinner. The only condition is that you must accept the answer. I started allowing my inner child to pick my clothes every Monday. Now, she buys everything. We eat a lot of chicken nuggets. There is a good reason why my hair is pink.

When we allow ourselves to experience life through the eyes of a child we are open to seeing the joy in the mundane. The beauty in the simplest things. Yellow sunflowers. Chocolate bars. Staring at a dog. Our heart bursts over and over again when we listen to what our heart loves and not what we think we should do.

You will be amazed how permission to play in even the smallest corners changes how you feel about yourself.

ABANDONED PLAYGROUND

When we first start this work, it can feel impossible to love ourselves. It is impossible to deny love to a child. A woman I worked with once described her body as a waterproof forcefield. Love had no hope of seeping through. Even though she was aware of her pain, she had no way to touch it. Until she met her inner child. By seeing herself so small and worthy of love, her inner child took on the role of a benevolent Trojan Horse. Throwing open the gates of her abandoned playground from the inside out.

You will grow to know this feeling well. Let your inner child mottle and warm where you are cold and closed.

Wise parenting never ends. There will never be a time you

won't have to be there for yourself. If you are willing to always grasp the hand of the child inside, you will unravel, and mend, together. By reparenting the Invisible Child, the Ghost Woman becomes more real. And in tending to her wounds, we begin the delicate work of facing the deep and ignored pain we have numbed for so long.

Once we shine enough light into the darkness, the thaw is on.

CHAPTER 10

Tundra

HOW TO THAW FROM EMOTIONAL FREEZE

Ice does not melt in sunlight
But in time

THE THAW

Ghost Women thrive on the black and white. On the all or the nothing. On hot ego-fueled love or the darkest of hatred. We have practiced cold aggression for a long time. The icing over was slow and insidious. Our disappearance was painful and long. Thawing from emotional freeze takes time. Do not expect anything faster than a slow burn. We cannot heal the way we were hunted. Settle for the middle ground. Gentleness is a lesson we are dying to learn.

If you throw a baby into the ocean and tell her to drink, it won't take long for her to drown. If you hand her a sippy cup, she will suck a little, and understand. Healing your internal cruelness is no different. To date, you have practiced ruling your kingdom through fear. Numb is all you know. And here you stand. Open to a new way. But bleeding, and afraid.

Give yourself a chance to be very bad at swimming. Don't expect self-love to rush and smother you. Love is impossible when you have spent your whole lives encased in black ice. Trying to love yourself quickly will send you back to hell dressed as a fraud.

Our bodies are breathing diaries chock full of painful memories. We hold deep, cold, and biting evidence in our bellies. We are aching on a cellular level. I only have to think about myself as a young child for my body to turn chilly and yearn for a hug.

Emotional freeze casts a long shadow across our whole lives. We have never allowed ourselves to feel anything other than inadequate. We have stuck a gun in our own backs. How could we possibly know anything about love?

This work is the softening of extremes. Ghost Women are poker-faced and unpracticed in the slushy mediocrity of honouring what we feel. We are guilty of overriding everything. Of just feeling okay. Instead, our lives are monochromatic and polar.

As you embrace the thaw, hold no expectation that you must do it perfectly, notice an immediate and marked difference, or feel a sudden soul-warming rush of self-love. Settle for simply accepting who you are today.

Worry about tomorrow tomorrow.

As you thaw from emotional freeze, allow yourself to be bad at everything, and practice anyway.

TO THE CORE

Gentleness is practiced. For years, Mondays were the day I started again. The day I recommitted to shrink again. The day I ate very little. The day I worked my body into the ground. Always the counter to a fat weekend. Always draped in shame.

I started my healing work by giving myself Mondays off. The only rule for the day was that I did not have to do anything except go to work and come home.

I remember the first Monday. Letting sunlight wake me up.

I walked to a small garden in the neighborhood.

I loved this place. So many memories from when I first met

my partner. Vines snaking around white stone columns. Dappled light.

I sat cross legged on the low stone wall with my notebook.

"What do I believe is true about me?"

It is harder to lie when you write by hand. The pressure on the paper. Something about the pen resting close to your skin.

I believe I am fat.

I believe no one will love me.

I believe I am a fraud.

I believe I will never be happy.

I am only worthy when I work hard.

I wrote them all down. Pages and pages and pages.

Hundreds of beliefs.

As I scanned with my short fingernail, I saw the threads weaving. Distilling down to core wounds.

I am not worthy of love.

I don't trust my body.

Deep rooted. Dark. Bodily. A part of me. Like cancer. Jumping from bowels to lungs to brain.

I always thought I was complicated. I thought I was broken one million different ways.

No. I was hurting two ways. Every way I struggled were branches of two core wounds. I was shocked. It felt hopeful. That was enough for today.

There is no need to do anything with new knowledge except let it sink in and take hold. We cannot just push through our frozen bodies and blossom like yellow daffodils at the first sight of spring sun. Our bodies don't feel safe because we have spent our lives throttling our voices, starving ourselves into submission, and numbing to mute our pain. Our mind plays the role of cruel dictator with ease. Our body may also be protecting us from deep and compacted trauma that we don't have the tools to process safely. Yet.

I worked with a woman who described a coffin-shaped force-field encasing her torso. Her body was water resistant to feeling. Numb was her safety net. When she did start to lean into her body, she felt black hands reaching up through her throat, pulling her voice down. Desperate pleading hands trying to protect a secret she was not yet safe to tell. She got there eventually with patience, breath work, and with bravery that floors me whenever I think of her.

For her, and for many, it is not a case of just deciding to feel okay. It is a practice of thawing in time. All Ghost Women can make their pain visible, but we must cast it under gentle light. We can thaw our freeze. It will not happen overnight.

EGO DEATH

We all want that big awakening. We all want that rib-cracking moment where our bones shake, the sky opens, and we emerge reborn. We are nothing and everything all at once! We have the body we always wanted! We don't eat until we are sick ever again!

In our dreams.

Healing has an average quality to it, which is difficult for women fortified by rules, numbers, and deadlines. We have mined ourselves dry. Frog marching ourselves towards what we believe makes us good enough. We are not used to softness, squishiness, or open timelines. Trusting the process is a novel idea and the path is paved with fear.

I was terrified that I would lose everything that made me remarkable if I softened my grip. I was terrified by the idea of no longer dieting. I was terrified by what people would say as I rolled around my life with low standards. *Fat. Lazy. Conceited.* Every ordinary woman and boring man I had quietly, or openly, shamed became the future I feared most.

Even if you want to heal, you will find yourself caught in an invisible war: drunk and in love with all that destroys you. It was always three o'clock in the morning for me. I would wake up hungry and consumed by black-and-white battles. *Who am I if I'm not perfect? I can't keep doing this. But what if I gain weight and people notice? I want to die. Does being kind mean I'll lose my sense of humour? Will I become a boring fuck? Can I love myself fat?*

There is no shame in fear. Ghost Women have a deep and bloody worthiness wound. Any fear that bubbles into our minds as we begin the long thaw is a surface-level expression of this wound.

Wound is a polite word for this gash in our soul that has deepened, and widened, and festered through years of earning our worth.

Do not ignore fear as you thaw. That would be hypocritical. Bring the fear along. Comfort it. Let it have a voice. But, for once, not the deciding vote.

BREADCRUMB

Fear wants you resting on a bed of nails. If you stay lying down, the nails will eventually pierce through your skin and bleed you to death. Sitting up, putting your hands down, and clambering off the bed isn't without pain either.

There is nothing painless about healing wounds that, up to this moment, define your identity. The wounds feel like you. You are enmeshed. You fear the loss of consistent suffering just as much as you fear what you may lose through healing. This is normal.

You've seen how the spider spins. You've shrunk. You've worn the masks. You've caged your beast. You've felt alone. A lot.

You are here now. Your pain has hibernated in your body for long enough.

Your soul is calling.

Let me go.

Honour the call.

It may feel untrue.

You can dream of sun in the heart of winter.

You are like a tiny animal creeping out of her hole to the dewy smell of spring. Bleary eyes blinking. Is it warm yet? Has the snow gone? Are there nuts in the bushes? You must create evidence you are safe to leave the hole by gathering bread-crumbs. A breadcrumb is a tiny piece of evidence, something that is so small you would miss it if you were not paying attention.

Gently does it. You are healing from a cold war. Your body does not trust you. You do not trust your body. You must pay attention to any moment, or fleeting feeling, or act of bravery that gives you evidence that you can thaw. A kind thought. Letting yourself sleep in. Eating without counting. Connecting with your inner child. Leaving work on time.

Gathering breadcrumbs is a powerful practice. You must allow yourself to feel the soft and gentle warmth of every single tiny breadcrumb that guides you across the bridge from invisible pain to embodied healing. No breadcrumb is too small to celebrate.

Your mind is practiced as a weapon.

Unload the gun. Learn to hold a wand.

CREATING SPACE

The first way to gather breadcrumbs is by creating space. When we are practiced in the art of self-violence, there is no space between who we are, the shrinking, the stories that we spin, the masks that we wear. We are bonded to our pain. To our fear. To our sadness. And the closeness blinds us. By taking a moment to detach from our feelings, we give ourselves space to breathe and observe what is present without making the pain personal.

Ghost Women are married to our thoughts and feelings. When I was numb, I would think about my weight and feel something uncomfortable like fear or guilt. Within seconds, I would eat something, choose to not eat, or start thinking about a diet, or count my calories for the day. I was a rubbish bin, constantly collecting uncomfortable feelings, and compacting them with hunger, food, or fear. Never once did I allow myself time to process or learn from the feeling. Never once did I create the space to understand the wound that was bubbling these feelings to the surface.

When we are bonded to our feelings, we are reactive and fast. We tie our identity to a momentary sensation and label ourselves as the emotion. Or the action we take to avoid the emotion. *I am worthless. I am greedy. I am ugly. I have no control.*

No wonder we are addicted to escaping ourselves. No wonder we dull the thoughts and feelings with anything, or anyone, we can get our hands on. We will do anything to glide like swans on glassy lakes. Pretending we are perfect.

Every feeling we have is not a referendum on who we are. It is a current of energy experienced in our bodies. It is information. There is no hierarchy to what we feel. Fear is as useful as joy and anxiety is as interesting as boredom. Our resting state is not happiness. Our resting state is being. When we cling to happiness, or recoil from sadness, we silently reinforce the black and white thinking that locked us in emotional freeze.

CAN YOU BECOME THE SPACE THAT HOLDS YOUR PAIN?

Imagine you are outer space. Deep and luminous darkness stretching to infinity. You have an endless capacity to hold all things. All sensations can exist in your endless space. The navy soulless sadness. The biggest joy. The cool and impatient fear. The fast and jumpy anxiety. The deepest love. The hot and amber anger.

These emotions are not you. They are the planets, the stars, and the asteroids. They are the black holes, the cold corners, and the rocky lumps that float in endless space. They will all pass, and disappear. But not before you learn their lesson.

When you notice an uncomfortable thought or feeling arising in your body, take a moment, lower your eyes, breathe into your belly, and feel that feeling sitting in you. A distinct and separate object within your endless space.

You are not the feeling. You are not the fear. You are the space this energy exists in. Allow the emotions to sit in space and allow yourself to watch closely, as you would a rare bird. Cultivating the power of observation versus identification will ease you into thaw. Gently ask the question, "What are you here to teach me?" and listen for the answer. The answer will reveal the wound that, in time, you will learn to tend.

SUSPENDING REALITY

The second way to gather breadcrumbs is by suspending reality. Ghost Women have learned the only way we can express pain cleanly is by shrinking. The choice to stop dieting and allowing yourself to eat without rules is not an easy choice. I had an encyclopedic knowledge of the nutritional breakdown of all food. I also had a lot of evidence that when I ate what I wanted I gorged for a week. Even when I knew I had to stop dieting, the fear that I would binge every time I ate something "bad" was terrifying. Until I had proof of the opposite, this story held me in a vice.

CRAVE

We are starving for something food will never satisfy. The only thing we need to commit to is allowing ourselves to eat.

I have heard it over and over again. Coming out of my mouth. Coming out of other Ghosts' mouths. "I'm addicted to sugar." I worked with one woman who could not stop talking about chocolate almonds and popcorn. She would mention them every week.

Her story shows the power, and the curse, of fake lack. When we make anything artificially scarce, we crave it. Love. Attention. Food. And even when we beat the urge to eat, craving fills our minds at the expense of all else. We believe we are addicted.

We are not addicted. We are experiencing fake scarcity.

There is no perfect way to stop dieting but start by not pathologizing food. Practice not using words to describe your eating that reinforce judgement or being wrong. No more diet, binge, portion, fasted, cheating, restrict, calories, macros, scales, weight, or carbohydrate. Just eating. This small switch will start to unwind the dieting judgements that loop unconsciously through your mind.

CAN YOU EAT THE ELEPHANT?

You will not stop dieting and immediately stop binging or wanting to restrict. You have to find the heart to let go, knowing that you will feel uncomfortable a thousand times before you feel normal around food.

One of the easiest ways to take the power out of food is to go toe to toe with the elephant. Eat it one bite at a time. One morning early on in my non-dieting life, I walked to a shop close to my work and bought a croissant. I spent time and let myself choose the one I wanted. Custard and cherry compote. I put it on a dark grey plate in the office kitchen, walked to my desk, and took a bite.

My teeth sank through the thick custard and crunched on the pastry. I felt the butter coat my lips. I held on to the joy for the short moments I knew I had. And then, like clockwork, the fear rose and quietly engulfed me. It was nine o'clock in the morning. And croissants were dangerous. *Banned.* Eating one signaled a binge.

At least, that was my story.

This was my moment. Could I stand here in this ocean of fear and be with myself? Could I gather a breadcrumb? I stood still. And I allowed myself to feel it all. To everyone in the office, I was eating breakfast by the window. Inside, I was traversing past lives of shame. Decades of pain. Flashbacks of the mornings I would shove food down my throat in the school toilets so fast I tasted blood. All the photos on my phone that I took every single week to check my progress. My tiny body. My big body. I saw me in the future. Fat and sad. And I wondered if that was what was waiting for me. A nightmare on the right side of kindness.

I stood there. And I kept chewing.

A whole life inventory because I ate a croissant for breakfast may sound crazy. But eating a croissant and feeling my feelings was an act of courage. Eating a croissant and then moving forward with my day and not eating 10,000 calories is a memory that, to this day, brings me to tears.

Every time we give ourselves permission to eat food, we are eating the elephant. And the elephant has nothing to do with food or our body. She is everything we project onto our body.

That elephant is a sight to be seen. Years of unworthiness. Years of not enough love. Years of shrinking. Years of abandonment. Years of shame. Years of trauma. Swallowed. Compacted. Compressed. I faced it all eating a cheap croissant.

We heal one bite at a time.

I know that is not the answer you want. You want to just be normal around food and do all the hard work quickly and be done with it. Yesterday would not be soon enough.

It does not work that way.

The bright side is it gets easier every day you take the power out of food. Acknowledging the elephant exists in the first place is half the elephant. And from there all you really have to do is eat her one bite at a time by removing any and all rules around food.

You will hit a tipping point with food when your body understands she is no longer fighting for her life. When you eat and stand with the emotions that arise, you chew through enough unworthiness, fear, and shame to realise you are safe to eat.

Trust generalizes.

I rarely eat croissants for breakfast anymore. That's a choice made in love, not fear. I can eat a croissant whenever the fuck I want. That is freedom I will never take for granted.

RESOURCING WISDOM

The third way to gather breadcrumbs is by borrowing bravery and wisdom. Ghost Women have brilliant minds. Our capacity to create realities is astounding. Unfortunately, we have used our wand as a weapon to build a tiny, fear-ridden universe where we are worthless. This is the small self at work. To expand our reality, we can gather breadcrumbs by resourcing wisdom from our Future Self.

CAN YOU LEAN ON YOUR HEALED HEART?

Positive affirmations barely sink into our skin before our body rejects them as foreign and fake. Embodying a vision is different. Bring your Future Self with you everywhere. Pretend, for a moment, you are already healed and act accordingly. Imagine you are someone who eats with ease. When you are fighting the desire to shrink, ask your Future Self what she thinks. Resource her fiery heat. Lean on the strength of her healed heart. Allow her knowledge to guide you like a star in a cloudy sky. In time, the gap between the hurting and healed self collapses.

WINTER SUN

Every winter has its tipping point. Where the snow turns slushy and muddied with dog paws and piss stains. The melted ice sinks into the earth creating a mucky thick slush. And a few hardy slabs of ice last until the July sun melts them into small rivers.

Parts of your pain will feel glacial. Ancient pain locked up in our bodies for a lifetime. Holding on, and holding out, until you prove you are ready to thaw.

All that glitters is not magic. Do not expect the thawing of your body to be beautiful. The overwhelming experience of healing is muted. Average. Beige.

Feel the gentle warmth of cold spring sun seep through your body. A soft and gentle reminder that you can rebirth. The ice will thaw as you hunt for breadcrumbs. And as you hunt for breadcrumbs, the ice thaws.

Suspend yourself in the promise of tomorrow. When you feel yourself creeping back into the hole to hibernate, find one tiny breadcrumb to keep your nose sticking above the soil's edge. Learn to breathe life into the parts of you that were sleeping. Over and over again.

By building a bridge with your body, you open the door to meet your shadows with light.

CHAPTER 11

Shadow

MAKING PEACE WITH SHAME

——

I would watch as my parents loved her
With an easiness, and a softness that I never knew
Her hand made for holding
Her heart open
I pretended I did not care
But I was watching
I saw all of it
Chewing on soft white bread as I choked on crusts
I would sneer at how much she needed them
I would have given my life to know her secrets

She was born off the hook
So comfortably middle of the road
She got the soft balls, the warm hugs, and the easy ride

Not from me
I existed to remind her of just how pointless she was
My words like knives

Stabbing her exactly where she was softest
Slow with sums
Clunky with words
You're so dumb you know
Quite useless
I threw my shadows black and thick all over her
She would just smile and say she wished she could be more like me

Easy to hate because she was so easy to love
And I was never that
All she ever wanted
Was for me to love her
I needed her to know how nothing she was
So that I could fill my heart with something

The shame tastes so delicious
So fatty, so meaty and warm
I could live on it for a lifetime

Little sister
I am so sorry
For the ways I was to you when I was fighting for my life
You don't have to
I hope it is okay
That I am trying to forgive myself

THE SHAME GRADIENT

Pull up a chair. It's about to get shameful. No human being does anything without purpose. There is a reason behind everything Ghost Women do. Even when our choices make no logical sense and are cruel or self-destructive. As you start to wake up to your pain, and see the tactics you chose to fight for your visibility, shame will walk through the door with relentless consistency. When you start to see how you hunted in all the wrong places, betrayed yourself, and hurt innocent people, the darkness may feel like it could swallow you whole.

All Ghost Women have a shameful shadow of the unforgivable, dirty, and unclean kind. Or so shame will have us believe. It is normal to feel mortified by what we have done. When our standards for ourselves are impossible, we act out of desperation with no regard for collateral damage. Nothing we do is all-the-way bad. We are not unforgivable. If we are committed to making our pain visible, we must learn to love our shadows as fiercely as our light.

Our bodies do not feel shame by degree. Shame has an uncanny ability to fill every crevice of our body with gloopy dread. It sits like stone in the stomach, chokes the lungs, and floods the veins with prickly acid. When we allow ourselves to feel terrible for the ways we chose to survive when we were fighting for our lives, shame wins. As we bathe our bodies in shame, we hear a loud whisper that we deserve to suffer for our badness.

You should have known better.

Shame reminds us that we are not neatly divided into good

and bad parts, or healed and unhealed parts. She knows no walls. Shame hangs over everything, like smog over a beautiful city. We may not choke and die as her dark fumes fill our lungs, but we will never thrive. We must find ways to make shame concrete and real so we can accept what we have done, and find a way to move on.

Like lies, there are a variety of things we feel shameful about. From the mildly bad to the downright cruel. Some shadows are easier to shine light on than others. In your quest for visibility, you must meet all corners of your shame. Find it inside to forgive yourself. All the way.

MUNDANE SHAME

Mundane Shame is the lowest grade of shame and, in some ways, the least complicated. It is any act that, in hindsight, feels embarrassing. Mundane Shame registers in the body as a low-grade fever. We may feel a ripple of embarrassment, but it rarely involves directly causing pain to someone else. The shame lies in the act itself.

I feel ashamed of the simple food-related crimes I committed. I will never forget the look on my mum's face when she came into my bedroom and saw a pint of ice cream dripping down the wall. I had passed out eating it.

I ate mouldy pizza out of the bin. I stole food from my roommate's bedroom in college. I went through her drawers when she was out and took her snacks. When I worked in cafes in Scotland, I spent the shift stealing food and eating behind the counter. I licked sugar off my fingers and served customers. Cold bacon lodged in my gullet. I used to walk to three different grocery stores on a Sunday night, buy boxes of cookies and chocolate bars and shove food in my mouth on the way home so my partner didn't notice how much I was eating.

Eating mouldy pizza is disgusting. It did not hurt anyone. Food was my lifeline. It was the drug that numbed a lifetime of pain. It gave me a moment to feel nothing. The feast and the famine was the clock I built my days around. Structure within my storm. Embarrassing, yes. Cruel and pointless? No.

When I grasped for something to save me, food caught me. Exercising until I couldn't walk caught me. Starving caught me. Numbing caught me. Shrinking caught me. In the way nothing else could.

You can heal Mundane Shame by admitting you didn't have the right tools to be with your pain. You had to numb somehow. So when you feel the first ripples of embarrassment, don't drown in a puddle. Ask a better question:

Why did I need to do this?

What am I not safe to feel?

What am I really hungry for?

Did anyone die?

By asking questions, we give ourselves the chance to understand that we did the best we could. We can also learn what we really needed in these shameful moments. The answer is rarely food. We are love-hungry. Rest-hungry. Fun-hungry. Worth-hungry. The answer lies in what shrinking gives us.

Never forget to ask if anyone died. The answer will always be no. And you might give yourself some much needed medicine. An upward curl of your lips.

Dare to smile at your shame.

Your soul will thank you.

OUTSIDE SHAME

Outside Shame is the projection of our shadow onto others. It encompasses all the ways Ghost Women cast our darkness, and make other people suffer to validate our superiority. Outside Shame is harder and darker than Mundane Shame.

The way I treated my little sister growing up is an example of this. Belittling overweight women is another. I could fill a graveyard with the corpses I slayed to make myself feel smart, superior, and funny.

I was quite talented at throwing my shame around. One summer in college, I was home in Scotland. Summers should have felt like a break from the brutality of being a collegiate athlete. I found them terrifying. No structure. No purpose. An easy time to get fat.

I would not allow it. I was waiting for our coach to send me my fitness program. In the meantime, I was filling my required exercise hours with endless running. Dreaming a hopeless dream that my legs would forget their DNA and shrink into the lean twigs so many of my teammates had.

My sister asked if she could join me.

I smiled to myself. This was going to be good.

We ran through the neighborhood to a quiet cul de sac.

"What are we doing?"

"You'll see."

I beat her into the ground. Brutal sprints. Lunging hundreds of yards. Burpees. I'd speed up as I lapped her for the fourth time.

"Move!"

She could barely walk for a week.

She never asked to join again.

Point proven. You're weak. I'm strong.

Looking back is hard.

I was hurting.

She had to hurt, too.

THE ENEMY

Outside Shame feels chilly and dispassionate. Our wounds cast willful ripples that engulf others in our painful crusade. There is no consent. Enrolling other people in our suffering is not something we do consciously. As you do our work, you will grow to learn how many people were collateral damage in your fight for visibility. Even those you love.

My grandpa was a major in the Second World War. This gentle kind man killed a lot of people because it was his job. Fighting for visibility is the Ghost Woman's war. We slaughter the enemy with ease by forgetting that they are also humans. That they are just another heart as incomplete as ours.

I have yet to meet someone who is rotten to the core. Some women I have worked with have, so use discernment. Almost every single person we meet is a mirror to gaze into. If another person brings out the worst in us, it is often an arrow pointing to where we are hurting most. Jealousy is intimately connected to Outside Shame. My sister's kind and chatty smiles stabbed my prickly, dark, and contrary wounds. She got what no one thought I needed. Obvious and generous love.

She had to pay.

The way other people dance in our emotions is a chance for reflection and learning. Outside Shame is a well-worn road. When you lash out and enroll someone in your suffering, take a moment to ask yourself these questions:

Are you a terrible person?

Why am I making you pay?

What do you have that I think I do not have?

What can I learn from you?

It was so clear to me that I could learn a million lessons from my sister. She walked me to the torn edges of my gaping wounds over and over again. So did every fat person I mocked.

If you are reliant on hurting others to feel strong, you will not suddenly stop. Practicing compassion towards yourself will soften your treatment of other people in time. It is also beautiful to offer a heartfelt apology. Even if the thought fills you with dread.

INSIDE SHAME

A dermoid cyst is a saclike growth that some women are born with. The sac contains teeth and hair. It grows quietly and anonymously. Part of us. Deeply embodied. But sometimes the cyst ruptures. If it does, you are in trouble. This is what Inside Shame feels like.

Inside Shame is the hardest and most difficult shame to sit with. It is a dense and dense and dark mass of interwoven stories, the masks we've worn, the fraudulence we've felt, the trauma we have survived, and the ways we've hunted ourselves. Inside Shame festers in our bad and unlovable parts and feels like a stabbing and hot assault on our identity. It does not require much activation. I would wake up at five o'clock in the morning on Mondays with Inside Shame choking me. The crime of being me was suffocating.

Mundane and Outside Shame are clues that lead us to discover our Inside Shame. They are the surface level expression of a Ghost Woman's wounds. Inside Shame is their source of endless energy.

Some parents are honest enough to admit that they love one of their children more than the others. They are brave. So are you. When you are learning how to sit with Inside Shame you have to acknowledge the parts of you that are hardest to love.

You may not like what you feel when you add all your shame together. We do not become more human by fragmenting the self. We cannot leave the parts we dislike on the floor.

I am not proud of making my sister feel stupid, shaming fat people, missing my grandpa's funeral for a diet, and stealing food from bins. I needed all these parts when I was fighting for my life.

Getting close to your darkness is not about holding a shame referendum. Believing we must always feel this way. Shame thrives in shadows and is healed by light. By naming our deepest shame we make it real. By making our dark parts real, we zap their power.

No witches need to burn at the stake. Bring your Inside Shame out to dance. By making your shame concrete and personal, you do the same for your whole self.

BLACK BLUSH

Shame feels like a black blush. She feeds on the lie that we should have known better. "Should" is just another chance for us to suffer under perfect's vicious reign. Ghost Women are not perfect women. Using our bodies to transmute our pain into strength and not caring who we stood on, or how deeply we lied was a bad strategy. Surviving was our greatest achievement. Casting shadows kept us alive.

We went to war with bad tools for a long time. As we start to make the darkness luminous, it is easy to shame the tactics we chose when we were desperate. Shame allows us to pretend that we should have known better.

We could not have known better.

Shame is not healed through more shame. Shame is not healed by avoidance. Shame is not healed by cutting out or disowning the parts of us where our darkness collects and pools. It takes bravery for a Ghost Woman to feel pathetic in a body that has mastered pretending to be strong. It takes guts to sit still and not find a way to numb the shame away.

You have guts.

SHAME BODY

Our Inside Shame is healed through awareness, acknowledgement, inclusion and then, perhaps, forgiveness. In time.

We have years, perhaps decades, of evidence to prove denial of truth renders us invisible. We must swell our capacity to hold the worst of us. We can use the power of Inside Shame to start a conversation with the parts of us that we would rather leave on the floor.

Start by making your shame human. Create a Shame Body. Separate her identity from yours. Give her a personality. Find a photograph to make her feel real.

Your Shame Body has a heatmap. Whenever you feel her black blush rising, welcome her. When she arrives at your door to pick you up, ask her to park the car and sit down beside you instead. Tell her you want to comfort her and learn from her. Do so by asking these questions:

Where in my body do you live?

What colour, texture, and temperature are you?

How long have you felt this way?

What do you believe you have done?

How can we heal together?

How can I love you more?

MAPPING

Shame rests in our cells. A woman I worked with described her Shame Body as a pit in her pancreas; rotten, black, and bleeding. She began to heal by sending love to her childhood self, and forgiving her mother. The love turned a key, unlocking her.

My Shame Body makes me sweat. A whole body fire. She is very young. Sitting in a classroom. Desperately trying to erase a handwriting mistake. Learning to decorate other people with nasty comments and white lies. I have learned she is calmed so easily with a reminder that she does not have to be perfect anymore.

One woman's Shame Body spoke with the voice of her domineering mother. It coursed through her every time she ate too much, and she cowered in its corner.

Another woman's Shame Body lived in the memory of what was done to her by a man who should have known better. Learning to be with, and heal, her shame was the ultimate fuck you to the unforgivable.

We fear most what we do not acknowledge. Keep a mental picture of your Shame Body and commit to mapping her darkness. Learn where she hides in you.

When she comes out to hunt, sit her down. Meet her with kindness. Shame is not healed through shame but through forgiveness.

Learning to sit with our Shame Body opens up space to include and transcend our pain. By speaking with darkness without denying its truth, we teach our bodies that we are listening.

From this place, forgiving the ways we were made to feel invisible is a lot easier.

Victimhood is comfortable. Are you ready to let go?

CHAPTER 12

Mother

WHY FORGIVENESS IS A
PERSONAL MERCY

———

Her face crumples and a tear falls. I have done it again.

She sits curled up against the side of a worn couch, her knees neatly tucked in under her frail and small body. Her left knee is thick and gnarled with arthritis. You can't tell under her mum trousers. Navy. A size too large. A cardigan of some sort. At least a couple of buttons. She was a ginger. Sturdy and smiley. I used to grab her arms and count her freckles. Her pink skin covered with brown flecks like all the stars you can't see in the sky. I would look at my skin. Sallow. Five freckles in total. Perhaps one mole. Unblemished. Not the same.

We live across the Atlantic from each other. Even sitting across from her in the living room I feel the distance in every way. Water desperately wanting to mingle with oil. Her hedgehog daughter. Prickly, snippy, but oh, so good.

She was never pushy. She saw everything I was capable of and gave me what she could. She came as close as I allowed. And I would see how her heart danced when I trotted over with another craft or project I had worked on to reveal something of what lived inside my head. A clue. A way for us to connect, if only for a moment, before we both returned to curling up on opposite edges of the couch.

We danced. Me sitting in corners and behind chairs. Small, and cold. Her pottering around reading her books. Rarely a cross word spoken. Rarely an honest one either. And I would catch her when she thought I was not watching. The flashes in her eyes looking at me like a thousand-piece puzzle, every piece the same colour. She could have screamed "Who are you?" and maybe it would have been better.

She never did. And I never made her. I just kept up my side. The number of times I sit and think about her. And I want to hear her voice, but I don't know how to ask for it. I feel gratitude and love and sorrow all wrapped up and around my body. I am half her, and yet a stranger. And it was not her fault. I made myself anything but easy. She never landed a hook in me. I know now it was not through lack of love.

She sits opposite me on what feels like a January day, but it could be October. I am about to go to the airport to disappear for another while. She sits. The knees curled. The hot water bottle nestled in her like a duck egg, warming her thin and aching bones.

And we are laughing. And I am playing my part. Evasive, cheeky. I'm prodding her in all the places where she does not look after her own heart. Her wayward daughter, her middle child again. All in black, poking at her. And she's laughing without her eyes, and brushing her bitten fingernails against her lips. A clue.

I cannot help it. A cat teasing a mouse. I am playing with her. And I know what I am doing.

And that's when her face crumples. Like a fissure through dry desert. And she starts to cry. And a deep noise comes from her throat. Like it has been there a while.

It is immediate. The wash of shame. Why the fuck do I do it? Why? What did she ever do but not quite know how to love a child who was waterproof to love?

I sit and watch her from the other side of the room. Frozen. I know I cannot hug her, because that is not what we do. I watch her and I hear someone saying "Mum, stop. Please don't cry. I was just playing with you. Please don't." And the voice is mine, but it feels outside of me.

I stay over here and watch her crumple. And I do nothing but say words to make myself feel better.

After too long, she stops crying. She sniffs briskly.

A hanky appears from inside her sleeve. I can see her filing it away as she gets up to grab the keys. We drive to the airport. And I leave for another year.

I send her an email later to say sorry. It's the only way I know.

I am sorry, Mum. It is the least I can say.

PLAYING VICTIM

Like kids on the playground, shame loves to play with blame. When the Ghost Woman is first waking up to her pain, the crisp taste of blame is enticing. Finger pointing. *You did this to me.* It is the most comfortable seat in the house. We are all guilty of bubble wrapping our victimhood in blame and staying there for too long. Blame is emotionally cheap and energetically expensive.

It would be so easy for us to make the curse of our invisible pain someone else's fault. To make why we shrink someone else's fault. It would be easy to throw up our hands, tell our story, and hear well-meaning people console our melodrama. The pressure release is palpable. "See, I wasn't fucked up. They were." Some Ghost Women have suffered terribly. Victims to heinous acts. Experiences you would not wish on a sworn enemy. I feel deeply for all women who have been betrayed, but I beg you.

Do not allow your life to turn into a memorial.

History cannot be erased. The roadmap of Invisible Child to Ghost Woman is imprinted on us. As awareness of the roles others played in our disappearance deepens, blame looks good to our hungry hearts.

We see the love we did not get. The belief deposits. The stories that spun. For some. Verbal, physical, and sexual abuse. The identity we crafted on the backs of lies. We see wrongness sitting outside of us. We pounce.

Could I make my pain my dad's fault because he didn't know how to express his feelings? Yes. Could I make it my mum's fault when she told me to suck my tummy in? Yes. Could I make this about the hockey coach who told me I played my best at 50 kilograms? Yes. Could the women I have worked with blame the men who raped them? Yes. Or blame the mother who decided she did not want to raise a child? Yes.

Blame is easy. It will not help make you whole.

The ways others hurt us are a projection of their own wounding. We have no control over their heart to heal. Blame does not help a Ghost Woman feel real. We can understand the reasons why we disappeared. Why pain did not register. The parts people played. We do not heal by compiling a list of grievances and expecting others to provide an apology.

We must take our power back. If we make our healing tick on someone else's timeline, and believe we cannot move forward without an apology, we could wait a lifetime. Dependency models are, by definition, disempowering. When we finally choose to give a real fuck about ourselves, we cannot rely on anyone outside of us to give us permission to proceed. We must march to our own beat. It is a chalky stone to bite. "Sorry" is not required for you to do your work.

Making other people responsible for why we continue to suffer leaves us victim to our past. Blame maintains our status as a victim of experiences that we had little control over. Even if we became complicit and active participants after the fact. It denies us access to freedom. It places the power of change outside of us. You deserve better. The liberation of the Ghost Woman is no one else's journey. We are solely responsible for healing how we hurt.

DAD

I was raised by an open but closed man. I am his daughter in every way. Strong legs planted, our weight sits close to the ground. Our sallow skin and dark eyes hood and sink in the same way when we are tired. Our brains move faster than others can follow. And real friends are not the easiest to come by.

My dad was the youngest son of two doctors. Intelligence is no guarantee of love. I did not know his side of the family well. They died suddenly when I was young. I am not sure they should have been parents. My dad never said much. By saying nothing, he said everything.

Hurt people hurt people. Physical scars are decoration. The wounding of emotional abandonment carves deep trenches in a human soul.

My mum once told me all my dad wanted was for us to feel loved. Every dreary grey Saturday he stood for hours on the sidelines of my hockey games watching quietly as I played with the heart of a lion. I was the best player on most fields by miles. He knew it. I felt his eyes on me always. There was never any pressure. He was not like other loud dads yelling about how good I was. He stored his pride for later.

My dad taught me how to work. He never said anything. I learned by watching. And I see it now. He hunts for his worth, too. When we were growing up, he rarely slept more than two hours each night. His attention sat silent and trapped behind an office door.

In the rambling debriefs on the car ride home, his love sat

so close to the surface it felt like an invasion. Every pass, every flick, and every sprint I had made. Stored away, and commemorated like an exquisite painting.

I cringed at his admiration. What should have been balm felt like vinegar. I wish I had known how to rub it in.

Hockey was the way my dad knew how to hold me. Today, I see him grasping for something to replace my hockey stick. So he can say I love you the only way he knows how.

I do not know if he saw how my gifts hunted me. How my perfection was forced. If he did, he did not know what to say.

We are not the only ones with bad tools. We have no right to blame anyone. This man loved me quietly on the sidelines. He held me in imperfect hands. It was not enough to stop me from disappearing, but my shrinking was not his fault. He was not held either.

No one ever gets all that they need.

That is why we need ourselves.

THE COST OF BLAME

There is a sliding scale to trauma. Sexual, physical, and emotional abuse are the unforgivable work of the deeply wounded. I was not a violated child. Many Ghost Women are not so lucky. I have seen forty-year-old women turn to stone when they revisit a memory of hearing their sister molested. Some childhood experiences are unforgettable, and the perpetrators unforgivable. But violation is not a requirement for trauma.

Life events do not have to rise to a specific bar to count. Many Ghost Women have not experienced a defining moment they can label as trauma, but the subtle pervasive suffering does not make it any less real. Your body holds the score. It decides what hurts you. That is why you must learn to listen.

One woman told me the story of a childhood friend dying in front of her and her dad. It was a freak tragedy. He never talked about it. Neither did she. Another woman was haunted by family members calling her adolescent body obscene. She found quiet ways not to eat. She knows her little girl notices when food disappears overnight.

Wounding is the dubious gift of coming into contact with other people. Family wounding runs deep like trenches through ocean beds. Whether we are conscious of it or not, trauma is so embedded into our sense of self that it informs every move we make. It colours every wound we slash into someone else, even when we care deeply for them.

Every human interaction is staged in the war ground of mutual wounding. How do we ever heal?

You did not have a choice then. You do now.

Will you sacrifice your life and remain a tragic and haunted monument of suffering? Will you slaughter the lamb over and over? Or will you choose to stand in the centre of your life and take ownership of your pain? Can you have the heart to include and transcend all that you have lived with, and through? Can you find a way to rise up?

A MAN I KNOW WELL

We all hold a lifeforce in our body. A certain amount of energy that creates how we are expressed in the world. At any given time, this energy is decentralized, tracking around our body like the complex tunnels that carry blood out of the heart. When Ghost Women lack awareness, our sense of self drains into sinkholes.

Sometimes, the skin's surface is punctured and we bleed. Pity.

Sometimes, the tunnels block, darken, and turn necrotic. Shame.

Sometimes, blood pools in pockets and organs. Fear.

Sometimes, we believe someone else's heart beat can beat for us. Worth.

And sometimes, our energy drains from us and into someone else. Blame.

This meandering feedback loop creates suffering. To plug our drains, we must disconnect from anyone we blame for having a hand in our disappearance. To re-establish our equilibrium, we must rip off the parasite.

Cutting cords with people and the past is a powerful way to stop energy draining into blame sinkholes. It can happen in an empty room and it does not require conversation.

Close your eyes. Visualize the person you want to cut cords with standing in front of you, attached to your stomach with a thick cord. Imagine an open channel. Feel the exchange of murky blood, pooling and darkening in their belly, slowly draining into theirs. Breathe into the hook they have in you. Let the memories flood back and forth through the channel. Do not judge the degree the pain must rise to. We can cut cords with quiet and loud pain. When you are ready, bring your hands to your stomach. Rip out the cord.

Ghost Women must understand that disconnecting from blame is a personal mercy and does not have to imply forgiveness. By surrendering our victimhood, we slowly draw our life force back into our bodies.

Do not underestimate the power of visualisation and breath. I have seen women weep on the ground as they forgive their dead mothers or cut cords with a room in their childhood home. You can cut cords with a specific situation without severing a whole relationship.

Through cord cutting, I have changed my relationship with my dad. This man I know well. I released all expectations of what a dad should be. I found ways to love him for who he is. A slightly awkward and brilliant introvert who sees me in a way that will never be repeated in all of history. I can now feel his love without thinking I missed out on something.

FORGIVING OURSELVES

Letting go of blame is one thing. Forgiving ourselves is another. It is normal for Ghost Women to resent what we have done. We have wasted years of our lives, lost and fighting the wrong war.

You have not missed a single second. When we are in hell, starving our bodies to feel strong makes twisted sense. Forgiving ourselves is a long process. It can start with a simple but vulnerable admission.

I was not perfect. I did the best that I could.

When you make your pain visible, you start to see the dreadful ways you scrambled around in your own darkness. You could point the finger. You could ridicule your dumb tactics. You could ladle shame on shame, lie down, and drown in it. You could wish for the years back. You could apologize for the rest of your life and never vanquish the pain you put yourself through.

Or you can find a way to let it go. You can surrender your impossible standards and admit you got it wrong. You got it very wrong. Find a way to sit by your own side anyway.

By softening into a more nurturing role, your treatment of other women may also change.

CHAPTER 13

Cunt

WHY WE MAKE WOMEN THE ENEMY

---

*I sat beside her. Not in person. In an online call. Healing
the modern way. In the matrix. Sitting on my own floor in
my own house. Sweating in heavy summer heat. Secret food
wrappers stuffed down the sides of chairs. Shameful choices
buried deep in bins. She was right next to me. My webcam
square pressed up against hers. If we were on a plane, I would
feel her fat nestling against my thigh.*

*I tilted my camera down to flatter my jaw. She had not. I
studied her face. It filled her square. That and the bridge of
broad shoulders. I could tell, and I was pleased. Fat, I thought.
She's really fat.*

*Talk about why you're here, the teacher said. I don't remember
what I said exactly, but I can guess. "I'm Iona. I have an
eating disorder." I loved this story. So convenient. Noble, too.
Disciplined, in my brokenness.*

Other women spoke. Perhaps six of them. One without her webcam on. I remember thinking she must be enormous. I found her online. Truly an elephant. I scanned the screen to check other weights. I was probably the second smallest woman. Fine.

It was her turn. I stared at this stranger somewhere in America. Curly hair, wiry with greys, and flat on top. I stared past her at her wallpaper. Yellowish. Old-fashioned frames around photos of people she must care about. Ugly curtains.

"I'm a doctor." That's embarrassing. This forty-something-year-old woman, blood vessels sprouting around her eyes.

Then she started telling her story.

I was sweating. Suddenly, I felt ice cold.

Because when she spoke, her story was exactly the same as mine.

The words were hurting her. Like chewing on bodies of dusty beetles. Her throat. Open after so many years. Truth spilling out.

I stared at her square in silence. Sweat in my hair, legs sticking to the wooden floor. But cold. Alone in my room. Surrounded by women. I listened as her fat mouth chewed and stumbled over her story of shame.

My story of shame.

All the same pain. All the same suffering. All the same guilt.

Like I was staring into a mirror.

I was furious. So much of me loved how special my precious suffering was.

At the same time, she set me free.

WOMEN HATER

There is a certain arrogance to Ghost Women. We work hard to create nightmares that we are too proud to share. Even in our bleakest moments, we love our white knuckles. We can use our tortured strength as proof of our superiority over other women. "At least I didn't give up like those fat bitches." Noting how flawed others are is much easier than looking in the mirror and bearing witness to the horror.

Ghost Women fear ourselves first. We fear other strong women second. And we feed on weak women third. Our sense of self is based on dominance and we fear any threat to our fragile house of cards. When we are deep in our pain, we believe the lie that all women are direct competition. That we're drinking from a finite pool. That their bodies, achievements, and gifts lessen our chance to be seen.

Self-hatred is a heavy burden for even the strongest spine. That's why we feast on other flesh. Projecting shame and judgement is a safe way for Ghost Women to voice what we fear most about ourselves. I used to love being a bitch. I got sick joy from judging other women. Too Type A if they had ambition, too fat if they ate normal meals, too vain if they cared about clothes and makeup, and weak if they talked about emotions. All the parts of me I hated or did not accept, I made their sin.

And I was a coward about it. I always hurled the axe in their back as they walked away. "You're whispering very loudly," people would say. I knew I was.

Women we see as weak become an easy target to boost a Ghost Woman's floundering ego. Their frailty bolsters us. In contrast, strong women threaten us and fill us with dread. Jealousy and judgement bite down hard. Their competence casts a shadow over us as we fight for scarce limelight. But as Ghost Women learn to cast light on our own shadows, our fear of other women stealing from finite worthiness pools eases.

Worth is not something you have to steal when you know it lives in you.

By being kinder to ourselves, we give other women permission to break open and heal.

DANCING GHOSTS

Special is a lie a Ghost Woman's ego loves to spin. We are not unique in our pain. My hockey coach once told me a story about lobsters. Thrown in boiling water, male lobsters built ladders with their claws to try to help each other escape. Female lobsters locked their claws together and held each other down. *If I die, you die.*

I do not know if the lobster story is true. I don't want to know. Because it feels true. I was not the only woman in my life feasting on weakness. I have held down other women. I have been held down. We all have. Other Ghosts Women have smelt my blood in their water. Taken what they needed. And left.

Time after time.

My best friend in college held me down in the most subtle and excruciating ways. We were both recruited to play field hockey at Syracuse University. As I floundered adapting to the overly sincere and fake-feeling American culture, her dry British sense of humour felt like home. She was a standout player. She quickly claimed a starring role, while I sat on the bench for the first time in my life.

She was better than me at hockey. That was the quiet and required undercurrent to our union. The rudder rode on a current of truth at first. She shone in pre-season. She got the post-match interviews. People knew her name around the field house. Our coaches loved her.

She was subtle with her words, but she made it quite clear how limited my skills were in comparison. I thought she was brilliant so I shut my mouth and took it.

I was working silently when nobody was watching. As she got the glory, I was learning just how far I could push myself in the gym. That was always the thing about me. I was stubborn and I craved the limelight. I had more than the glint of a starting position feeding me. All the extra running sliced fat off me by the week.

My best friend did not know it. But she chose the wrong Ghost Woman to fuck with.

Over months that bled into years, I watched her fall apart. Headaches to excuse average performances. Small injuries breaking her body. Every week something else.

Not my doing, but perhaps I did not help.

She fell from a coach's favourite to a nobody. She didn't get to travel for games. One season, she stopped brushing her hair.

It grew matted and dirty on her head, a dreadlock snaking up from the nape of her neck. She laughed it off, but fake smiles never quite reach eyes. People asked me if she was okay. I shrugged; I didn't know. Neither of us could talk about feelings.

She went home to England at Christmastime and came back with normal hair. We never talked about it. When she sat out one spring due to a shoulder surgery, I took her position in the middle of the defense.

As she weakened, I grew stronger.

In our final year, she returned for pre-season, fainted during a fitness test, smacked her head on the side of the track and was medically disqualified. My heart broke with her as she sat and cried gently. I did love her deeply. She was the best friend I had ever known.

But I felt electric. I had spent my summer living in a house with male cross country runners. I learned a lot about starving from them. I would eat almost nothing, train for hours on the track, then lie down and sleep to escape the hunger. I had learned to ride my silent pain perfectly.

She and I. We brushed quiet shoulders and I took what was mine. I played a standout final season. I binged and starved my way through it. To everyone watching, I was sublime.

That was the end of our friendship. She hated me overnight. I felt heavy guilt about how brightly I was shining. And she made it clear she had no space for my happiness and I don't blame her. She was in hell, but I still wonder. *Did you ever care about me in the first place?*

She started feeling scary. I would come home to her banging her head against the wall. It was impossible to be around her. I graduated and never saw her again.

Over the years, her story of invisible pain dripped out. Pure in its darkness. Almost deadly at times. She talked about it openly long before I ever put words to mine.

I am in awe of her. How far she has come. We even spoke a few times when I started doing my work. But years later, her wounds still feel fresh in me.

I mourn our friendship. Those years were special. Brutal and wrought like two hands grasping around a straining neck.

I've rarely felt so alive since.

She and I. We were fucked up together.

But it felt real.

I thought I had found the friend of a lifetime. Now, I see so clearly that we were Ghost Women dancing in each other's darkness.

You may feel special and alone in your pain.

You are not special.

For so long, I thought only I knew what it felt like to hunt myself. Feeding on my own flesh to prove something. To feel anything. To earn my own love.

I see it so clearly now. I was not alone. She was right there by my side. Hiding in plain sight. A Ghost Woman. A different flavour of invisibility. Tearing me bone from bone.

INVISIBLE ARMY

You are one small star in this black sky. Once you bear witness to your own invisible pain, you will see other Ghost Women everywhere. A cast of endless mirrors passing through your waking moments. There is an army of women that fight every morning to prove that they deserve to wake up. We bump impatient shoulders in expensive coffee shops. We race down opposite sides of the street as the sun rises. Breath billowing in cold hair. We x-ray each other with judgmental eyes. Searching for more bones. We suck in our stomachs with a hateful collective inhale.

This is why women hurt other women. When there is scarcity of space for us to feel significant, we lash out to mark our turf. When our distorted expressions collide, we wound each other in our fight to feel strong. Ghost Women are complicit in orchestrating our mutual invisibility. We imprint our unworthiness on each other, and unconsciously follow each other's lead.

The Ghost Woman's pain does not fabricate in a vacuum. There are forces at play that contribute to the power of our internal hunter. Our society celebrates the brink. No one escapes the dangled carrot that hard work will reward us with. That fat is the physical expression of laziness, rest is for the weak, and food is earned.

Our womanhood takes a pounding under this paradigm.

Only Ghost Women can give ourselves, and each other, the permission to feel real. We heal each other by creating the space to be truthful and by bearing witness to each other's pain.

The fat old woman on my first group call did that for me. She took a step outside of her shame and used her voice. I didn't feel that way at the time. I was outraged. How could this lazy woman be like me? How could she struggle in the ways I did? I was nothing like her. I was young, smart, and talented. Complicated. One of a kind. My pain was rich and vicious and mine.

In her honesty, she helped me take the power out of my pain. She taught me a valuable lesson.

You are not that special.

As I watched her chins tremble with truth that sounded a lot like mine, I realised I was her. Unremarkable. Almost Mundane. She was me. This was her pain. And mine. We shared it. And there was more to go around.

MIRROR, MIRROR

Learning how to connect with other strong women is challenging if the common ground you occupy is feeding on each other, or mutual prey. When I loosened my grip around my own neck, I realized that we are all trying to win the game with a bad hand. We have no idea how to play without fighting.

As we thaw from emotional freeze, we must learn how to

take responsibility for our emotions by taming our inner bitch, learning how to look in the mirror, and finding the bravery to let go of dead wood.

PUSSYCAT

Ghost Women think we are complex beings. We are. But most of the time, our needs are basic. We want to feel safe and significant. If you walk down a city street, you will pass by hundreds of scared, lonely, and bleeding Ghost Women scampering around desperately trying to meet a baseline of safety.

When we are wounded, we hunt and feed silently on other women and their succulent weakness. Teardowns have cheap benefits. On days when the voices in my head were too loud, I spent my day judging every woman I met. Bitchy asides were a perfect pressure release. My bloodthirsty self-loathing needed a surface to burst through. It was easier if it was not my own skin.

Like a needle in my arm. Temporary release.

There was a degree of pride to my cruelness. I waved it off as a Scottish thing. But being a cunt is not a Scottish thing. It is a Ghost remnant.

I DON'T THINK ABOUT YOU

I saw her most mornings at the gym. She was a rich bitch. I remember someone showing me her dad on the internet. A millionaire. She did group workouts and had private sessions every day with at least one trainer.

She moved horribly. Pudgy and thick in the wrong places. I thought it was funny.

I don't remember saying anything to her other than, "Hi." She did not have a good body and she was not even close to topping me on any leaderboards, so I was not interested, or threatened.

One day, as I was leaving, she followed me up the stairs.

"Iona, can I ask you something?"

I turned around.

"Why do you hate me?"

I was taken aback. I spent five minutes assuring her I did not hate her. Then I left.

That night, after my second training session, I sat in the changing room laughing about it with some other women.

"I don't even think about that bitch."

It felt powerful. I must be good at killing people with my eyes.

It also felt wrong.

I was raised to be kind. I was no longer kind.

We do everything for a reason. Hurting her met a need. When we choose to do our work, being a cunt loses all appeal, but we often have no awareness of what cruelty gave us. We need to know so we can plant a kinder replacement.

To understand our drivers, we must first observe them. Start by noticing when your Inner Bitch shows up. When and where do you find yourself hunting for ways to feel good by making other women feel pathetic?

My pattern was simple. When I felt fat or out of control, I hunted to kill.

Do not shame your Inner Bitch. She is a practiced response to unworthiness. Instead, turn her over and imagine stroking her belly like a pussycat. Ask her why she doesn't feel safe, and listen for the answer.

Start a list to scour for patterns. Often, the Inner Bitch is very young. Your inner child stretching her vocal chords. Learn how to diffuse her venom by asking why she is hungry for someone else's blood. Learn how to mix with this shadow. She will soften in time.

When we choose to turn towards ourselves with curiosity, you may hit unexpected gold: respect and compassion for other women. Start practicing kindness by noticing beautiful things about people you would normally shame. Many Ghost Women are fatphobic. I was. I had to actively counter my violence. When I started my healing work, I made a commitment to internally heal my fear of fatness. Now, I never compliment weight loss. I never remark on weight gain. All comments on bodies are off limits.

Another uncomfortable truth.

You must stop commenting on bodies if you believe all women deserve to be seen.

SALT SHAKER

We all know women who are easy to hate. Something about how they mingle with us grates our nerves like parmesan. In my mid-twenties, I worked with a woman who felt like fingernails. Her shrill voice. Her fixation on rules. Her inability to think creatively or take feedback. A dazed elastic-band smile, medicated and stretched across her pointed face.

She spent her day in spreadsheets. Pouring caffeine down her thin throat. Her tiny body drowning in a hoodie. The type of body that makes leggings look baggy. I would feel her breathing next to me in meetings. Her presence made my skin crawl.

It is human nature to hold ourselves up against another person and make them wrong. When we are healing, Ghost Women can learn a lot about compassion by staring in the devil's mirror.

This woman was my lesson. A practice in tolerance.

The people who stab our systems are our greatest teachers. Every day, we have the chance to gaze into someone's eyes and question why they make our blood boil, flood us with jealousy, or cut us so deeply. It takes practice to suspend judgement long enough to take the lesson. Pause and imagine that a small, trembling child is standing in front of you. A child who didn't get the right kind of love. *Just like me.* Just like you.

Ghost Women are not special. We are not the only ones who did not get our needs met. We are not the only ones with bad tools. We are all fighting invisible wars.

You know this firsthand. Be better. Be kinder. You are modeling kindness for other frozen hearts.

Other people can also show us where we have not healed enough, or accepted ourselves fully. I often feel the dull ache of jealousy when I see other women thriving in powerful, creative leadership positions. Standing on stages. Using their voice. A part of me still wants to shame their stage makeup and their girly clothes.

Use the way others make you feel to trace your core wounds. Imagine your whole body as raw skin. The person in front of you is shaking salt all over you.

Where is the salt gathering and clumping? Other women often made me feel jealous. Jealousy was not the core wound.

Below jealousy lay fear: You are taking light away from me.

Below fear lay scarcity: Praise is finite.

Below scarcity lay love: I don't get what I need.

Below love, lay the core wound.

Worth. I am not worthy of love if I am not perfect.

Notice how the core wound traces up and through to the surface.

It is so easy to hate someone for having what we crave, or for making our skin crawl. I never quite found a way to like the elastic-band woman. But I was able to bear witness to her flavour of genius. Her brain held a library of technical details that bored me to tears. She was incredible at her job. Whenever I felt judgement rising when she didn't see the world my way, I imagined catching glimpses of her as a tiny girl. A mousy face peeking out of holes wondering if she was safe to come out before disappearing away. Scurrying and scared.

Her own pain. Unprocessed and pure.

Who am I to judge?

Who are you to? Be better. Your healing depends on it. Allow yourself to stare into mirrors every day, trace your wounds, and start mining your gold.

DEAD WOOD

Trees are a beautiful metaphor for healing. When you trim back their bowing branches, the tree straightens. Shooting skywards. Trimming also stimulates her root system to deepen into fresh earth. She grows taller. Both above, and below, the surface.

Through this work, Ghost Women can do the same.

Healing can be painful and accompanied by loss. We can learn from the worst of people. But some mirrors are not worth our time. Some people do not have our best interests at heart. Some soil is barren. Some flowers just want to be weeds. And the hardest one? Some just aren't ready.

Thawing from emotional freeze can be a lonely road if those who you surround yourself with are not ready to bloom.

Women you had a lot in common with may turn into big obstacles and painful reminders of who you once were. Give everyone a fair chance. But you must not allow those unwilling to grow to stunt you. Cut the dead wood that weighs you down.

Trust in letting go that you are creating space for fresh roots.

I met another woman through work. She was twenty years older than me and striking. Dark hair. Sparkling eyes. A deep knowing. It felt like she had lived a million lives. Lightning storms lived in her. She'd talk a lot about feeling people and their energy like she was tapped into a different circuit.

I didn't really get it.

She was wildly supportive of me. My designs. My presentation skills. My critical thinking. She was always generous with her praise, but I kept her distant because it sometimes felt like she was looking through me. Seeing things.

It was not safe to know her.

I filed her away as cool but a wacko.

Until I broke and started doing my work.

And there she was. Open arms. Like she'd been waiting for me.

One night, we were out drinking wine and eating nori dusted fries.

"I didn't used to think you were beautiful."

I felt it sink through me.

She had a way of saying honest things.

"The other women thought you were. Your body. But I didn't see it. You were closed and dark."

She paused.

"Now, you're open."

I felt the tears streaming down my face.

I was not ready for her when we first met.

I was ready now.

NEVER FORGET

We attract what we radiate. As you become a beacon for vulnerability and emotional honesty, your ecosystem will shift to mirror your healing. It is not just other Ghost Women who will feel your healing. The way you shine your light and learn to dance in your shadow gives the thirsty what they crave: permission.

See how relationships that are meant to stay deepen. Parents. Siblings. Partners. Taproots cast down into healing souls. See the flowers of friendships bloom. Welcome our courageous women in with all their colour, glitter, and grit.

Let forgiveness floor you. Ask for it from those you have hurt. Do not expect a response. Be open to receive when it is offered. The same teammate I sliced and diced on the bus in college became a dear friend years later. I don't know why she forgave me, but she did.

We can even laugh about it now.

But we never forget where we came from.

What we have both lived through.

Know this, too. Growth does not land without pain, and a forest may burn along your walk home. People will leave you. Mourn the destruction, while planting hope. You can come alive amidst the embers of a forest fire.

NOW, BLOOM

Ghost Women. We have been quiet for too long. And our silence makes us cruel. It keeps us precious, unique, and separate in our experience of pain. Our fear keeps other women pinned.

We must do better. For ourselves. For each other. We have been complicit in our collective suppression for too long.

Burst the dam.

We have hurt each other. We can heal each other. Ghost after Ghost after Ghost.

Unmuting. Like whispers on gold window panes.

A voice of something real. A desire to be seen. To be honest.

After all this time.

Do not underestimate the permission you give to other women by choosing to live with a clean and open heart.

By liberating the pain that keeps you small, you heal the past, the present, and the future.

CHAPTER 14

Blood

WHY HEALING IS A SELFLESS ACT

———

I don't know how you will need me
I will do my best
To read your life by moonlight
Not through hard eyes
Your tiny hand
Wraps a vice around my heart
I do not know the ways you will cry out
But I will know I did my work
Forged in love
Raised in mud
I hope you never build
The walls of perfect around your mind
Or learn to feel careful about your smile
I will watch
For the ways you are strong
And remind you wax can melt
Beaming through a slatted window
Your soft skin aglow

Like you caught and kept a layer of sunlight
For when the shadows come
And I know
She will meet them in the parks
Down the street
In the corners of classrooms
The little women
Of other brave mothers
From broken jigsaw puzzles
The gluing together of tiny souls
No ghosts play on this open grass
This is the dance
Of mended blood

HEIRLOOM

Pain runs in families. Seeping through the oily pore of generations. Every Ghost Woman's journey is personal, but our disappearance is the result of an unconscious collaborative effort. Set in motion long before we were born. You are not the first woman in your family to feel the biting pain of invisible suffering. You are not the first woman too strong for your own good. You are not the first woman to go to war with your body. You are not the first woman to shrink.

You are no more, and no less than the current expression of your bloodline. Which leaves you with choice resting in your hands. Any healing Ghost Women accomplish is felt by future generations. Do not pass your invisibility forward. Do not allow inherited pain to run you over as it leaks and lusts for fresh bodies and younger terrain.

Have the heart to heal.

The health of our bloodlines is like a wild river ecosystem. Frogs jump from stone to flat stone. Insects hum in the moments before a frog's tongue zaps them. The water is glassy and clear, sheep graze the grasses and drink, and their wool grows soft and warm for a farmer's jumper.

This is a healthy river. But with the shifting of tides, our bloodlines muddy, thicken, and stagnate. Loss, grief, tragedy. Pushed down. Compacted. When we do not have tools to process our emotions, we dam our pain, and our bloodlines start to stink. Trauma frozen in time, passed down into the cells that become you.

Frogs droop sunken on their stones. Flies drop into murky

water. The farmer goes hungry. His fields scattered, morning after morning, with another flea-ridden corpse. Dying from the same silent virus.

Our bloodlines are no different. There is no absolute predictor of suffering. The healthy and the rotten bloodlines are not demarcated by wealth, by colour, by creed, or if the family unit is broken or intact. There are families tilted towards health, and families tilted towards certain expressions of pain.

Sludge sits in the memories of what our people have not had the heart, or tools, to clear. Pain heirlooms weave through family fabrics. Memories. Trauma. Pain. Most of what we inherit we cannot hold in our hands.

TOO BIG

Do not believe for one second that you are the first Ghost Woman to carry your family name. One summer, I visited my gran in a nursing home. She came out of the bathroom, her underwear at her ankles. She had forgotten. Her brain was spongy and dumb with dementia. All her sparkle had faded.

I knelt down and pulled her thin stockings and underwear up to her waist. She felt like a broken bird. Easily snapped. Withering under layers of wool in summer. I could smell urine on her clothes.

We walked outside in the sun. I sat down beside her on a bench. Her shoulders slumped. She said nothing. She was too embarrassed to talk. I think she knew her mind was dying.

Then I felt her bony finger prodding my thigh. "Big," she said. "Too big."

I swallowed hard. I was thinking the same thing.

I still wonder who jabbed their index finger into her.

INHERITANCE

The ways Ghost Women suffer are deep-rooted, learned, and shared. Our bodies hold the scores of battles that we did not choose to fight. We are the latest embodied expression of inheritance. The love, the light, the gifts, and the pain. We mirror and reflect what we see. What we were born into. We outflank and take over their war. We fight as they did, and still do. *Quiet. Invisible.*

"I learned this from my mother." I've had countless grown women weep in front of me. "I don't want this for my daughter." I know they mean it.

Many don't come back.

Every choice we make breathes new life into looping fingerprints. If we do not choose a new way, we are wiring our system to replicate the pain that ran into us. We are bringing another generation of Ghost Women to bear.

I know that this work is not easy. You have endured far worse, so we must find it. However deep you have to dig. You must find the heart to heal.

RIPPLE

Many Ghost Women have a fast fixation with how uniquely painful and personal their story is. A part of us does not want to share. When we only focus on ourselves, we miss the world. We have skin in this game beyond the borders of self. Do not underestimate how interconnected your choices are to the far-flung corners of your own universe. You may feel like a drop in the ocean. You are not a drop.

You are a ripple.

When we heal, a ripple forms. Small and faint at first, and in time so strong she flows backwards and forwards through generations. A mighty wave who whispers, then booms. *I'm ending this pain for us all.* Backwards and forwards. A ripple to a mighty wave.

And so. When I choose a new way, I heal my sister, my mum, my gran. I heal the stranger in a black-and-white photo. I do not know her name, but our eyes crease the same when we smile. I heal the cheeky, sparkly daughter I may or may not hold in my arms. When I choose to quiet the darkness roiling in my blood, my heart beats differently. One hundred years from now, a wee girl with thick eyebrows and short curly hair feels the difference.

Do you have the heart to make your domino fall differently?

When we choose to make our pain real, Ghost Women we do not heal in silos. We are lighthouses. We become living and breathing embodiments of truth, and we roll this healing forward and back through time and space.

Sometimes, it is beyond hard to be brave. To do what feels

like the work of your life. The vulnerability is painful. Sometimes, your own inspiration is not enough. Your Future Self is not inspiring, your Inner Child has nothing to say, and you slip into old habits. Mindlessly counting calories and slating your ugliness in the mirror.

In these moments, Ghost Women can find strength by resting on the hearts of others.

I started to heal my invisible war soon after my brother told me he was going to be a dad. I knew in my bones it was a girl. She flipped a switch in me. This child was not my daughter. We live in different countries. But I would die if she drank my poison. Her birth made my work urgent. Unselfish. I could not let this tiny soul grow up cast in my shadows.

She was born as I was mending. I will never forget seeing her for the first time. Her tiny body pressed against mine. Like medicine. I am so grateful she is here. On the days I need it, she helps me beat my own heart.

DOMINO DAUGHTER

Perhaps you are already a mother. Perhaps you don't want children. It does not matter. When you do not feel strong, a daughter, real or otherwise, can ground your healing in a broader mission. When our own heartbeat is weak or slow, feeling into how our choices may impact our daughters and future generations can light compassionate fire within us.

I am not a mother yet. But I have a daughter I have created in my mind. Her name is Fin. I think about how I would have held her hand too tightly a few years ago. What I would have said about bodies. About smallness. About work. The ways she would shrink because of me.

It makes me dangerously sad and equally hopeful because I have infinite influence over how this domino falls.

Do not try to be a perfect mother. I know Fin will not get out of childhood unscathed. Focus on how you want to love someone who is half of you. Who is born with a similar bent. Who still pumps some tainted blood. Who might try to disappear the same ways you did.

Make a list of things you will never teach her. I have promised my daughter will never see me counting or weighing my food, or my body. She will never hear me talking poorly about fat people. I will watch for when she is strong. Reach out for her hand over and over again.

And I will remind her that she is not alone. I will teach her how to lose. She will learn her gifts don't earn her worth. That she is loved by default because she is alive. And if I feel old patterns grinding gears in my mind, I will have the awareness to lean on my healing.

This daughter is an expression of you. Tangled in your legs. Real or make believe. Imagine a day could dawn when you hold her hand and tell her, wide-eyed, about the work you did to change her life.

A GAME OF DEGREES

It is a lot to stand in the middle of your life and feel how it fractures endlessly. Healing beyond ourselves and changing the course of your gene expression may sound like the claim of a crazy person.

You are only one brave choice away.

Imagine you are at a single point in time. Your whole life is suspended in this single moment. You can continue the way you always have. The way of the Ghost Woman. Or you can shift one degree to the left and start walking. This shift could encompass a macro or micro choice. It could be as large as the choice to heal or not to heal. Or as small and apparently insignificant as an in-the-moment decision to honour your aching body and not go for a run. To eat bravely in response to hunger.

In the grand scheme of a foot, your choice is insignificant. You miss your old target by inches. After a mile, you miss your target by a hundred feet. And if you fly to the sun, you'll miss it by a million miles.

One degree. One different choice. One entirely different life. For you. And for all the women who come after you. Every time you take a brave step, you shift your needle in the orientation of healing.

A couple of degrees were the difference between the Titanic hitting or missing the iceberg. A game-time decision. A more assertive choice.

Don't sink on this ship. Healing invisibility is not a big moment. It is the day-to-day following of the breadcrumbs that lead you to a life you could never have imagined was possible.

THE COST OF NOT

Ghost Women are part of a web of the ways things have always been. You are a tiny node within a network that is listening. What happens when you start sending out a different signal? Unlooping the blueprint. Spinning with different threads.

You have the power to change lives beyond your own. It is a choice.

You do not have to do this work.

Not today, and not ever. You can carry on creating your pain. You can act out the storyline someone else wrote for you. You can shrink in shadows. You can keep your eyes closed, hum a quiet tune, and let someone else bear this burden.

This is not to shame. This is to acknowledge that healing is not easy. Sometimes, it takes years for flowers to bloom. Some seeds planted we won't live to see in this lifetime.

Know this. Any work you do to breathe health into your bloodline is a gift. It is the work of a selfless woman.

Will you say it?

This ends with me.

You are cleaning your blood. You are claiming your north. You are reorienting your ship. When your domino falls differently, you set in motion a clattering chorus of women not scared to be seen.

Stand up. For you. For her. For them. Let your ripple roll. For that curly-haired child a century from now whose giggles sound a lot like yours, whose eyes sparkle a familiar and mischievous glint. She may not know your name, but she will feel your healing. Her bones will know how brave you were. And the woman in the old black-and-white photo, brown with time and soft on the corners. Who had no way to voice the way her body was violated. She will feel the benefits of your work, too. She will thank you for opening her mouth.

Forward and backwards. A rippling bloodline.

These are the choices we make. To rest on what we have always known. Or to learn to live a new way.

When you learn the tools to rise through your pain, you will never break. Even when life hurts.

CHAPTER 15

Bamboo

BUILDING EMOTIONAL RESILIENCE

———

He has a bent for sadness
It rolls through him in yearly tides
Waxing and waning by some dark moon
I can see when the devil is dancing on him
Turning all the keys in his mind
Believing
He is nothing

One hot summer
I decided
This heart
My heart
Must heal

But I was too scared to ask
Was his heart willing, too?

Mine

Slowly
Weeping ice
Learning
To pump my blood
Kindly

Not his

Clock hands spinning as the leaves fell off the trees

A closing over
A quietness
You can love a man
And also know when
It is not sinking through their skin

Then
Quietness

Then
Nothing

It happened over weeks
I watched him disappear
Into a blackness so thick, so dark
His face crumpled
Eyes gone

Grabbing his hand
Pulling him back home
Everything on a slant
The shelves
The floor

My heart broke
For him

And my heart broke
Again
Harder
For me

Like waves crashing on war-torn rocks
The pain smacked me about
My whole body underwater
Wintry numbness in its wake

And I clung to my heart
In chunks
Raw, blue, and bleeding
In quivering hands
Floating
In the misery
In the openness

Is his love
What healing will cost me?

The work
It will not make you waterproof
Swallowing an ocean
Is a surefire way
To drown

All of it
I felt all of it

It took time

The leaves
Icey and crisp
Mint blue skies
Scarlet sunsets
Tossed by tides
So much more time
Than I wanted
Then one day
I felt our feet hit solid ground

I watch him still
Quiet hours and long days
He brings me to different tears
The ways he has learned
He is not nothing

Where he hurts sits a little closer to the surface
Acknowledged gently now
Held with words
He did not know before
A different set of keys

The smile
I feel it hit the bottom of my heart
When my back is turned
The heart that whispered through me across a dark room
The night we met

A remembering
A fragment of me in him

My hand in his
Moonstone squinting in hot sun
I will wear it forever
If I don't
I sleep at night
Because I know
When storms break
I float

WATERPROOF

Healing invisible pain is not something Ghost Women can muscle through. The outcome of doing the work is not white-knuckled happiness. Setbacks, life events, and moments entirely out of your depth and control will roll your way. Expecting that healing invisible suffering will make you waterproof to pain lacks grounding in reality. You miss the point entirely.

The difference between a Ghost Woman and a Brave Woman is flexibility. By creating a supple sense of self, we transcend the rigid perfectionism that kept us numb. By putting our healing to the test in the moments that matter the most, we develop the awareness not to shrink. And the resilience to bend and flow.

Healing from invisibility does not make you waterproof to pain. The pursuit of permanent happiness is a convenient myth. Perhaps it gets you through the door. The desire for a more net-positive experience of life. Making happiness the definition of work well done is an oversimplification of your journey. Permanent happiness is not the outcome of making pain visible. The art of being is.

Like a storm over open water. Soupy and oceanic pain will roll over you. And you will not see it coming. People die. Relationships end. Bodies change. Friends let you down. You will let yourself down. Betrayal snakes her path through you.

Pain is not a failure. This is life. These are the moments where we put our healing to the test.

THE PHILOSOPHER

Ghost Women can evolve our lopsided definition of strength by focusing on swelling our capacity to hold all our emotions and experiences. Especially the difficult kind.

When I stopped dieting, it was not a fairytale. As I practiced eating normally, my cheeks puffed with sugar and salt as I practiced taking the power out of food. Dread pulled me through the floor as I sat on the toilet, blood in my underwear.

A woman of sorts, again.

Crossing the bridge to a more honest life is not without loss. Sometimes, it felt like a death. I mourned myself. The lilting beauty of ferocious fear. I missed them. The deep roadmaps of veins weaving an intoxicating promise of freedom across my stomach and down my arms. Bouncy fat pillows under thin skin. I watched as a small but needed layer filled in my jutting edges. Shrinking in reverse. I felt it all. The grief. The fear. The loss of self.

I did not rush it. It sat on me for months. Low-grade dread mixed with hope.

Living through the sometimes brutal hum of learning, and testing, emotional honesty is the making of us. The baking of the bread. Healing our invisible pain would be quite simple if knowledge was all we needed. Ghost Women don't lack brains. It would be nice if we could change our lives in a white room through the power of thought.

For many of us, this is often where pain hides. Trapped on the inside, tossing and turning in our minds. Or we give up on day three because learning to feel is hard. As if we have not endured far worse.

If you approach your healing like philosophy, you will never do the real work. You will stay an academic in an ivory tower. It does not matter how deeply you understand the complex underweaving that made you invisible. That caused you to shrink.

Reading about healing is better than denial. You must be willing to make a move. In the real world. The only way we make ourselves real is by becoming a brave practitioner. Speaking our pain aloud. Using it as rocket fuel for our transformation.

ONE SMALL THING

Mastery is the enemy of the good. Rumination is the enemy of revolution. When we add too much flower to the investigation of ourselves, we miss the point. We become poets of our story, but not embodied practitioners of the work.

When I first started healing, I wrote catalogues of suffering. How many more stories and connections could I find to understand why I was the way I was? Every day felt like a crime scene investigation. The pinning of memories. The piecing together of me. It was a good start. That's all it was.

As you become aware of a new breadcrumb of understanding, do not file it away for another day. Move with intent. Do one small thing that shifts you forward.

Make it so easy to win.

Eat a normal breakfast after a binge. Choose to go for a beautiful walk when you wake up bleary and tired. Right hand on your stomach. Left hand on your heart. Breathe. Even if it's just three minutes. When you catch yourself casually twisting in the mirror to assess your waist, at least smile while you do it. Ask a better question. Make a gut decision. Don't hold back your tears when they build up behind your eyes.

Every choice has energy attached to it. Cast your eyes on the horizon and trust true north. You are undertaking the recalibration of your body. Allow your heart to tremor with the hope of a new way. Beat by brave beat.

BAMBOO

Resilience and strength are not the same. In the way a bamboo shoot is not like a metal rod. One bends in the wind. Cut down, it regrows like new. Metal is machine-made, smeared with chemicals, and will always succumb to the rotting power of weather in time. Never forget it. You are living in the real world now. And you cannot heal the way you were hunted. Practice resilience rather than strength to help you embody the difference between a perfect healing journey and an honest one.

I don't care how well you do your work. The money you invest. How much you do each day.

Perfect made our bones brittle. Strong led us to suffering. If we are not careful, we will quietly redirect our rules and mea-surements onto "good things." We can meditate twice a day, read one million beautiful books, and attune to hunger cues.

But what happens when you miss a day of healing? How do you respond to what feels like failure?

I will tell you. And mark these words.

Do not turn your back. Now is not the time to shrink.

Begin again. Over and over.

Nothing will change if this work stays on the surface of your skin. Do not get lost focusing on the act of doing things right rather the art of being and feeling things deeply. This is no different than shoehorning your body into a small number and hoping that, by freak luck, you will find happiness and peace. Enlightened slavery will leave you in the dark. And very, very tired.

Your pain was born from one hundred shoulds and have tos. Bled into you. Bound by biting twine. Not good enough is the Ghost Women's chorus. A relentless drumming.

Even as you emerge from your hunger, keen and open, you will find yourself quietly humming her song. Have the heart to stop measuring your worth. To stop judging your life on a system based on less or more. Perfect, or broken. If the number is wrong, you are wrong. And the rusty drain pipe pushes a little harder on your throat.

Lives are not perfect. Lives are lived. They do not unfold on forced timelines through fake means. Healing is no different. We must have the patience to let our souls breathe us back to life. We do that by feeling. Unlearning. And forgiving. Over and over again.

It is a choice every day. To learn to bend in the wind in the most gentle and kind way possible. To be open to nothing at all being exactly what you need. Your soul is whispering.

Let me go.

Be thoughtful about how you bring your strength to bear in your desire to feel real. This lifeforce inside you does not need walls. Your spirit does not need more rules wrapped around her, no matter how enlightened they feel. She wants to flow like molasses. Sleep a whole day. Dig her feet in dirt. Seep into the corners of questions. Be all together poorly behaved. Fill a room with laughter.

Do not turn this work into another plundering of your soul. Yet another way to pull out the measuring tape or the calculator.

Learn instead to read the breeze. And bend like bamboo.

Our lives move on with or without us caring. It won't always go your way. We do not live in labs. We do not control the weather. We do not have the final say on the way other people react when they bump into us in the world.

We do not always get to practice breathing enough. We don't always have a chance to slow down. Wrought with tiny frustrations and inconveniences. Shaken by big, life-breaking moments. Or the days we wake up and feel like we've forgotten who we are.

You will fuck up. Those you love will fuck up.

We grow real on the battlefield. In all the moments of being a human. We have a choice. Shrink back and swallow your feelings. Berate your weakness. Numb until you're dumb. Or choose to build your capacity to bend.

THE ARTIST

Pain is inevitable. It is not the point. Do not strive to become a tenured professor. You are creating your future, and pain is rocket fuel. Don't sit on it and wait to explode. Let lessons move through you as you experience the raw joy of freedom.

We are here to live. With as open a heart as we can. Keep your eyes on the light. Commit to bathing your soul in freedom. Even when it is not easy. Crack a whopper of a smile and mean it.

Come alive like a dried chili soaked in water.

When we live more emotionally honest lives, our soul starts weaving through us. Filling the spaces where control used to hold us in vice. Like a drop of pink ink seeping through a cup of cool water. Learning to live in colour after years of black and white.

If you believe it always has to hurt, it will. Choose a new way. Make this journey a work of art.

I am an artist. I worked as a creative director. I have designed other peoples' visions and dreams for so long. Much of it is beautiful. But the work of my life? The work that brings me to my knees. It is me.

The work I have done to be me.

In every single moment. The gluing together of broken pieces. My whole self. My whole soul. And so much yet to learn.

Time is passing either way. Choose brave. Render this Ghost Woman real. Solid. Full colour.

You are an artist. The creator of your future. Everything you desire already exists. The woman who seems so far away is already here. She is already in you. Waiting. Perhaps not so patiently. Grasp her hand and run towards what you know is there. Somewhere.

Put aside perfect. Because perfect has no business measuring souls. Every day we take action in the absence of evidence, we make ourselves visible. Grow to marvel at your honesty and vulnerability. Put your work to the test with the people in your life who matter the most. Learn to dance with the unhealed blood. You will fall short of who you wish you were over and over again. Stand up. Try again.

A LOVE STORY

I have always known I wanted to marry my partner. He is American, but he felt like home. His rugged skin dusted with freckles. His wiry beard, speckled with ginger and white. Young but old like memories. His strong athletic body. Such masculine grace. He did not fawn over my Scottish accent. Or trot out the whiskey and kilt jokes that bored me to tears.

He had me. All of me.

He loved my mind. I would hear him talking about me to friends with a sense of wonder that made me burn. He saw me in ways no one else could. He saw me in ways I was not ready to see.

He would beckon me over. *Look at this beautiful photo of you!* Blurry, in-the-moment grins and scowls. Awkward angles. My face askew. The kind of photos I would pretend did not exist and delete.

He commented on boring things like a random tree or name-less mountains. He pored over maps. *Look, this is where we are in the world!* I loved him for it. But I did not know how to look up or around me in wonder.

My eyes only looked at him, or in mirrors. Chanting cruel trance. I could feel myself clinging. Hanging on his words. Keeping him happy. Hoping he would never leave me. And take his certain beam of sunlight with him.

I needed his love, because I had so little for myself. My confidence rattled and left as my body fattened and shrunk. I got quiet.

I was sand. Nothing built on me could last. We came apart a few times. But like magnets, we could not let each other go.

I saw the way he struggled, too. Flashes of anger. Swampy and cold sadness sat on him for months at a time. A bowing of the head. Eyes cast down. Embarrassment when he scrambled numbers and letters.

The shiny things that caught me in the first few months

lost their luster. He did not see the world the way I did. He always made the decisions. Even if he asked, I shrugged. You choose. I did not want to risk being wrong. For fear that he would leave.

And not just leave and come back like clockwork.

Leave for good.

My wounds open. I could not believe a man so beautiful was with me. I clung to a future he could not see. And sometimes this gentle man with the soft smile and light eyes was not kind. It was okay. It felt better than alone.

Until my reckoning came. I had no choice but to be brave.

I could no longer be the woman he met.

I don't pray. I whispered silently to no one so many mornings, afternoons, and nights. *I hope we survive my healing.*

The more I sat with my own pain, the more I saw his. I found myself watching him. Wondering if he added or took away my shine. Only for my love to roar back in as he twinkled the way no one else ever could.

I felt his sadness. What he lived with. In a way I was not awake to before. Sometimes a puddle. Sometimes cold, and dark, and scary.

And I wondered. Was this what life with me did to someone?

Some days, I would leave for work, close the door behind me, jump on my bike, and yell my tears into the wind. I did not care who saw or who heard.

His sadness? My pain? My body could not tell.

It felt like a lesson. A milestone. A chance to bend without breaking. Could I honour my healing and feel his hell? Could I give the man I loved the time to rise? Could I let him leave me if he had to?

I did.

I stood still. In space. I did not try to be strong. And I did everything I could to understand myself anew. And understand this man I loved anew. It took everything I had learned and practiced in easier moments.

Every way I had learned to not shrink.

EMOTIONAL BALANCING

You do not control your life. You will never know a whole person. The day they wake up and leave you. The day your dad dies. A car hits your dog. You lose your job. A friend cuts you off. You wake up sad for no reason.

You cannot calm the whole ocean. You can fill your lungs and learn to dive. Learning how to sit with pure pain, rather than manufactured suffering, builds emotional resilience. And you can learn ways to comfort yourself as you move through the hardest lessons. Emotional balancing is the practice of supporting pure pain with a courageous counter, like joy, love, or peace.

When we are hurting, it is so easy to believe that pain is all we can feel. That we are the pain. This can leave us feeling drained and hopeless. It is also an artifact of black-and-white thinking.

The grounding principle of emotional balancing is the concept of both/and. That we can be both deeply in pain, and hopeful. That we can feel shame, and loved still.

Mastering the art of emotional balancing will increase your tolerance to endure, and move, through pain. When we have been numb for so long, we have to practice.

Close your eyes. Imagine you are a desert, swelling your capacity to hold an ocean. Allow the pain to wash all over you without asking it to leave. After a few minutes, welcome in a valiant resource. Something to balance the pain. This could be a memory, your Future Self, or even a happy inner child. Turn the volume of the valiant resource up so it can stand like a beacon in the darkness.

Imagine this light beaming through dark water. Like shafts of light penetrating the deepest and murkiest layers of the ocean. Feel the mingling of light and the pain and notice how your body starts to relax knowing that it is held.

We can be both wildly sad and endlessly hopeful. We just have to be brave enough to try.

Movement is another potent way to fully feel. Pick your three favourite songs. Name the most present emotion in your body: fear, love, anxiety. Give it a colour. Then let your body express the emotion. This is not a dance. Move in whatever way feels good. Shake like a wounded animal. Crawl on the floor if you have to. Do all you can to climb out of your head and into your body. You will not feel instantly better. You will feel something. And that in itself is a miracle.

MOONSTONE

By choosing not to numb, you allow the pain to leave once you have grown through it. The fear I felt about losing my relationship sat all over me. I felt half shut. Dread pressing down. I stood quietly and let the storm rage through me. I leaned on my truth. I leaned on my heart. I leaned on my healed blood. And I leaned on the woman I was creating in every moment I stood still.

I gave my partner permission to meet himself, in his own time. To learn if he loved me still. I trusted that even if he left me, that I would not leave my side.

It took time. I learned this.

You cannot burn a house down when it is home.

He started to share more of what he really felt. His own strain of invisible pain. His own web. His own freeze. His own thaw. He started speaking with words I had only just learned to wrap around myself. It blew me away.

The clouds clearing. His laugh filtering through quiet moments. Back to the maps, and the weird history, and the silliness. Watching our dog and cat fight for his attention. I understand their jealousy. His love does feel that good.

He came back to me changed. Wiser somehow. A little more at home.

And on the days when I was feeling lost. *I am proud of you.*

His voice will always pull a thread in my heart.

It is hard for strong women to speak. Quiet men are no different.

When he bent down on one knee and asked me to be his wife. The moonstone winking and dancing in the early morning sunshine. It felt like more than a proposal.

We stand together now because we were different versions of brave. I can rest on his love in a way I never could before. I hope he knows he can forever rest on mine.

I know this, too. The only love I can ever guarantee is my own. He could leave me tomorrow. I don't think he will. He could.

That is why I continue to do my work. If that day comes, I know it will hurt. And I know I will be fine. Because unlike before, I am on my side. I can stand in storms. I am my home.

I may bend. I will never break.

THE PROMISE

There is nothing special about me. There is nothing special about you. Just a choice. And I hope you make the brave one.

So, one day, you will know what it feels like to stand in awe of yourself.

Some days, my body brings me to tears. Still. Even now.

In a different way from the days I would stand half naked in the gym bathroom. And take photos front, back, and side. The smell of moldy towels mixed with some guy's sweat thick in my lungs.

In a different way from the days I would bike home wobbly and lightheaded after crushing my body under a barbell and shovel brussels sprouts down my throat so fast I gagged. And go to bed, my tiny body lean and hungry with an alien binge bump in the middle of it.

Pregnant with the dread of tomorrow.

In a different way from the days after I decided to never diet again. And my body grew, and I would watch replays from my group program, study my pig cheeks, and guess how fat the other women on the call were.

In a different way from the days my body lost weight and settled. And I ate real meals. And had actual food in my house. Dumbfounded by how easy it was.

There are days. Weeks still. When I realize I am avoiding my body. Avoiding myself. Quietly shrinking.

I fear, even though I do not diet, that my body is not relatable. No matter how little I exercise in comparison to the glory days, this armour won't melt.

These are the moments when my body brings me to tears.

After all I have done. After all the ways I fucked her over. All the years I shrunk to the bone.

She stands with me. And we console each other. Not perfect. Not strong. Just here. Doing our best.

A work of art. Forged and battle-tested and healed by love and gentleness.

No more Ghost Woman.

No more perfect.

No more shrinking.

I want this for you.

More than you could ever know.

But this work is yours to do.

I hope you make the brave choice.

Darkness led you to this door.

Through pain that had to exist.

That broke you exactly in the moment you were ready.

And here you stand.

Everlong

———

Do not mourn the loss of years
Do not wonder what could have been
There is no start
There is no end
Just every day
The droopy quietness of dawns
The closing of the sun
Days where nothing happens
Nights where ice thaws
Take it all
And stay
And when you frighten
Stay
Slow mountains
Are moving
Ink dripping through
Space
Memory rendered real
Solid
Full colour

Tear stained
But giggling
This body
A scrapbook
Of all you have done
To be here
Breathing still
With joy in your bones
More often than not
An expression of your choices
The cruel and the brave

DO THE WORK

I want to thank you. For spending time with me. Hearing me spill my guts, learning about what I know can heal you.

It is your turn now. It is your turn to make your pain visible. To walk the long road home to yourself. To stop shrinking.

And you will not do that by reading this book.

This book may shine light on dark corners. It may turn something around in your head so you can see yourself more clearly. Some of my words might cut a little too close to your bones. Good. I've done my part.

It is your turn now.

I know there is a lot here. To help, I've picked out some of the most important truths from each chapter.

I SEE YOU

Sometimes it takes a Ghost to see another Ghost. **And I see you.** I see straight through you. Not in the way you want. In the way that you need. You don't have to be strong here. No talent, and no gift, no tiny number on the scale, and no capacity for work is wide or deep enough to hold you together anymore.

Brilliance, strength, and natural ability have a cruel way of making your humanity disappear. To make a woman like you feel invisible. Hopeless. And wrong.

Stay long enough with me to know you are not broken.

GHOST: WHY YOUR PAIN IS INVISIBLE TO OTHERS

When you are good at everything, you never earn the right to struggle. At some point when you were young, you were confronted by your limitations. No one else noticed. You disappeared in the moments where the perception of those watching sat at clear odds with the reality of your internal experience. On the outside, nothing changed. Internally, you felt the first tug of incompleteness.

These moments foreshadow the development of a tolerance for struggle and pain most humans cannot imagine. Your sense of self fractured. The Ghost Woman was born.

RECKONING: WHEN PERFECT WOMEN BREAK

Your day will come. You will wake up and realize the pain of being you is no longer a pain you can endure. I wish it were different. Your life may have to fall apart for you to finally pay attention.

I know it feels like you cannot be vulnerable. I know in the rest of your life you must be strong. I can hold you. Nothing you feel is too dark, too wrong, or too shameful. Vulnerability is the key that will unlock you. Allow yourself to fall apart with me.

BONE: WHY WE GO TO WAR WITH OUR BODY

Over the years, you turn to your body as the canvas to scream your invisible pain. By trying to shrink your body, you become more visible. It seems counterintuitive. But the smaller the body, the more space you take up. The more attention you get. The more real you feel.

The first master Ghost Women bow to is acknowledgement. A small body is the way you display your work in a form that strengthens, rather than weakens, you. The second master you bow to is either the curation, or numbing, of pain.

You cope through two channels. You blow the face off a volcano and binge until you feel nothing. Or you redirect the pain towards your body and feed on it, instead of food.

SPIDER: OUR IDENTITY IS A WEB OF UNTRUTHS

Identity is a way to wrap structure around the slippery, formless, and undulating magic of the human spirit. As a young child, your identity is created by stories spun about you, long before you have a voice of dissent.

A story repeated often enough becomes truth. It is not long before you become an active participant in cementing your identity. Even though it hurts. Over time, the separation between the spun story and your sense of self disappears completely. The stories eat through your soul like worms through a rotten apple.

WOLF: WE FEAR BEING DISCOVERED A FRAUD

Ghost Women live their lives feeling like frauds. We are terrified others will realise how ordinary we are. We learn to work very hard to get as far away from facing ourselves as possible. We externalize every single ounce of our worth.

Our deep fear of being discovered a fraud is fought by a jubilant and healthy knowing that we are very gifted. Our aching need to lie down and rest for a moment is countered by an inability to stop working. The polarity pulls us to pieces. We are both the hunter, and the hunted.

MASK: THE WAYS WE HIDE SO NO ONE HURTS US

You develop a complex array of masks to protect and hide your true self. In time, you learn how to slip into your roles unconsciously. Your audience falls for the illusion that what you let them see is who you are.

If you want to heal, you must peel your masks off. This process hurts and is accompanied by loss. You will mourn the intoxicating parts that made you feel special, dark, or different. For every weed we yank, we leave fresh soil for more of who you are deep down to bloom.

BEAST: WE FEAR OUR BODY'S BETRAYAL

You see emotionality as a wild lion you must control at any, and all, costs. Feelings are dangerous. You have learned there is nothing worse than a hysterical woman. You have no space in your life for anything that weakens you.

Emotions and vulnerability are not weak. Vulnerability is your greatest strength. You must learn how to feel and process pain if you want to heal. In time, you will learn who you are without the fear that keeps you quiet and sad in the corner.

GOD: YOU HOLD ALL THE CARDS

Learn how to suspend yourself in a space where you have already healed. Create a vision of yourself a year from now. You can do this through the Future Self Projection. In time, and with bravery, the gap between the hurting and healed self collapses.

It may seem like the road is long, and the destination is far away. There is nowhere to go. The freedom you desire already exists. The wisdom, too. Your only job is to peel away the stories, struggle, pain, and fear that made you deaf to your truth.

Stay still. Learn to feel. And listen.

You are the tiny bird tweeting.

You are the open palm twitching.

Learn not to crush your own bones.

CHILD: LEARNING TO PARENT YOURSELF

Your inner child is an unconscious part of you that stores your earliest memories. When she feels safe and loved, she is a conduit of creativity, intuition, and play. Often, your inner child feels unsafe, abandoned, or ignored.

It can be hard to love yourself. It is impossible to deny love to a child. Reparenting your inner child is a chance for you to practice. Learn how to reach out a hand, ask her what she needs, and learn to see the world through her eyes. By spending time with the youngest parts of you, you will strengthen your internal sense of safety.

TUNDRA: HOW TO THAW FROM EMOTIONAL FREEZE

I know you want that big awakening. Because you thrive on the black and white. On the all or the nothing. On hot ego-fueled love or the darkest of hatred. You have practiced cold aggression for a long time. But healing has an average quality to it. Settle for the middle ground. Thawing from emotional freeze is a slow burn.

SHADOW: MAKING PEACE WITH SHAME

As you wake up to your pain, you will see how you hunted in all the wrong places, betrayed yourself, and hurt innocent people. Shame will come knocking. It takes bravery to feel pathetic in a body that can pretend to be strong so well. If you are committed to healing your invisible pain, you must have the bravery to meet shame head on.

Create a heatmap of your body to learn where shame lives in you. Swell your capacity to hold the worst truths. Through acknowledgement, shame falls away.

MOTHER: WHY FORGIVENESS IS A PERSONAL MERCY

Do not become a victim to your past. Blame is pointless

and has no guarantee of ownership, or apology. It places the power to change outside of you. It is time to take your freedom into your own hands.

Cutting cords with people and the past is a powerful way to stop energy draining into blame sinkholes. By surrendering your victimhood, you draw your life force back into your body. You become more whole.

CUNT: WHY WE MAKE WOMEN THE ENEMY

Your sense of self is based on demonstrating competence and superiority over other women. Don't forget the story of the female lobsters. Women get good at holding each other down.

Do not shame your Inner Bitch. She is a practiced response to unworthiness. Turn her over and imagine stroking her belly like pussycat. Learn how to diffuse her venom. Mix with her shadow. She will soften in time.

Women have hurt each other. We can heal together. When you learn to lead with a brave and open heart, you give others permission to do the same.

BLOOD: WHY HEALING IS A SELFLESS ACT

Your journey is personal, but you have also inherited pain from your lineage. You are not the first woman in your family too strong for her own good. You are not the first woman to go to war with your body. So you have a choice. Will you pass the pain forward? Or will you have the heart to heal?

Healing is not done all at once but in tiny ripples. Start by making one brave choice every day. Every time you choose the bold path rather than numbing with perfectionism, over-working, or starving, you shift the needle in the orientation of healing.

BAMBOO: BUILDING EMOTIONAL RESILIENCE

You cannot heal the way you were hunted. Learn to focus on resilience rather than strength to help you embody the difference between a perfect healing journey and an honest one. Channel bamboo, not cold steel.

You are not an archaeologist of your past. You are a creator of your future. Your greatest achievement is this work. The work you do to render yourself real. In every single moment. The gluing together of broken pieces.

Your whole self. Your whole soul. And know that you are never done.

When the pain feels beyond you. Mark these words.

Now is not the time to shrink.

START SMALL

I don't preach roads I have not walked. If I'm sharing something in this book, I have run it through my body a few hundred times to ensure it has merit.

That it holds strong when I say it delivers.

That your time is well spent listening.

For these short moments that we have together.

You are your own answer. Do not blindly take my word, or anyone else's word, on what will set you free. Do not paralyze yourself with knowledge and opinions.

Find what you need. Go deep with what resonates. Stay a while. Practice. Get wise.

We cannot microwave wisdom. Gold is slow cooked.

Nothing I have shared is new to you. It is all a remembering. The stirring of dormant wisdom, asleep all these years, smothered by your invisible pain.

Time is passing with or without you.

Do not wait another moment.

Get your skin in this game.

Relearn your wisdom.

Do not get sidetracked by glitter.

By new and shiny ideas or a quippy line.

Glitter won't crack you open.

You will. What you practice every day will.

You do not need more knowledge. Not 101 books, 379 quotes,

lots of money, the right amount of sleep, everyone else's opinions, and the perfect moment to heal.

You need yourself. A dawned day. And a willing heart.

Run this book through your body and feel what is important. Take what you need and leave the rest.

The wisest woman in every room you walk into bears your name.

All the wisdom you will ever need. Here all along. Waiting quietly. For you to be brave.

Start small. Grow tall.

Iona

I want to hear your stories.

info@ionaholloway.com

"There is a vitality, a life force, a quickening that is translated through you into action, and there is only one of you in all time, this expression is unique, and if you block it, it will never exist through any other medium; and be lost. The world will not have it. It is not your business to determine how good it is, not how it compares with other expression. It is your business to keep it yours clearly and directly, to keep the channel open. You do not even have to believe in yourself or your work. You have to keep open and aware directly to the urges that motivate you. Keep the channel open."

—MARTHA GRAHAM

Acknowledgements

I want to thank:

My mum, Joyce.

My dad, Alan.

My brother, Andrew.

My sister, Heather.

My sister-in-law, Nicola.

I am sorry if this book was hard to read. I hope you understand. I love you all.

My niece, Evie. Thank you for giving me such a happy reason to do my work.

My partner, Sean. I know I am not the woman you met a few years ago. You are not the same man either. Thank you for growing with me.

My pets, Taki the Shiba and Rue the Cat. My pet-in-law, Lyla. You taught me a lot about taking naps.

Meghan McCracken. Thank you for saving me from a 7-Eleven book deal.

Jen Shaw. Thank you for sharing your love of bacon fat.

Ange Bradley. You gave me a chance without ever seeing me play. I will always run through the line because of you.

Liz McInerney. Thanks for sitting down on the pavement with me and giving me a second chance.

Leonie Geyer. Thank you for helping me through some dark years.

Joe Gillius and Karis Leckie. You understood me in ways no one else could. Thank you for seeing me.

My gran and grandpa Quigley. Thank you for the twinkly eyes and for breaking that plate.

The Scribe Team. Thank you for making this book possible.

All the women and men who have trusted me to help support their healing work. Thank you for being brave.

And last, but not least. To the moment I chose to begin this work. The slow moments in all the quiet corners. The wee hours. The tears and the pain. When I did the best I could. And the moments where I broke. And the moments when I realized I am never broken. To the teachers who showed me I am the teacher. To the friends who appeared when I was ready.

And to all the times it feels like I am going backwards. Until I remember I choose where I walk. To the light streaming through this window with a story to tell about something. Living where the days have no numbers.

Bare feet in the dirt. The drum of my heart. The smell of thunder, and a hint of Highland rain.

I am open. I am listening. I cannot wait for what is coming my way.

About the author

———

IONA HOLLOWAY is an author, coach, and speaker. She helps women stop shrinking their bodies, worth, and power through vulnerability, creativity, and breathwork so they can reclaim their lives and honour their gifts. She and her partner, Sean, live in Boston with a very clingy Shiba Inu and a cat Iona has never held. Her pets have taught her a lot about embodied trauma.

You can learn more about Iona at ionaholloway.com.

CPSIA information can be obtained
at www.ICGtesting.com
Printed in the USA
LVHW022226190121
676894LV00008B/1602